SCRIPTURAL PRAYERS FOR WOMEN

Transform Your Life Through Powerful Prayer

MEGAN PROVANCE

Unless otherwise indicated, all Scripture quotations are taken from the *King James Version* of the Bible.

Scripture quotations marked (NKJV) are taken from *The New King James Version®* NKJV®. Copyright © 1979, 1980, 1982, Thomas Nelson, Inc. All rights reserved.

Scripture quotations marked (NIV) are taken from the *Holy Bible, New International Version®*. NIV ®. Copyright © 1973, 1978, 1984 by The International Bible Society. Used by permission of Zondervan Publishing House. All rights reserved.

Previously Published as:
Scriptural Prayers for Every Day Life for Women
ISBN 978-0-9842534-1-8

Scriptural Prayers for Women
ISBN: 978-1-949106-95-4

P.O. Box 701403
Tulsa, Oklahoma 74170

Published by Word and Spirit Publishing
P.O. Box 701403
Tulsa, Oklahoma 74170

26 25 24 23 22 10 9 8 7 6 5 4 3

Contents

I. Growing In My Relationship With God

Start the Day Right. 2

God is my Hope. 4

God Loves Me This I Know 6

The Greater One in Me 8

The Gift of the Holy Spirit 10

My Strong Tower, My Refuge. 12

Dwelling in the Secret Place 14

God Complete Your Work in Me 16

Prayer of Contentment 18

Being Thankful. 20

Praise and Worship 22

Loving Myself as God Loves Me 24

End the Day Strong 26

II. Growing In God

Growing Up Spiritually 30

Craving God. 32

A Women of Faithfulness 34

A Fervent Women of Prayer. 36

I Can Be the Woman God Says I Am 38

A Proverbs Woman 40

Being Comfortable with My Body 42

Balance In My Life. 44

Refreshing My Mind with God's Word. 46

Saying God's Words. 48

Finding My Purpose In Life. 50

Lord Show Yourself Strong 52

Having a Character Like God 54

Rejoicing in the Lord. 56

III. When You Need...

Confidence . . . 60

Courage . . . 63

Discernment . . . 65

Faith . . . 67

Guidance . . . 69

Healing . . . 71

Integrity . . . 73

Patience . . . 75

To Control My Emotions . . . 78

To Simplify My Life . . . 80

To Have A Better Self Image . . . 82

Strength for Battle . . . 84

Wisdom . . . 86

IV. When You Are Facing...

A Crisis 90

Discouragement. 92

Fatigue in my Body 95

Fear in Your Life. 97

Procrastination. 99

Rejection from Others 101

Spiritual Drought. 103

Stress. 105

Growing Older 107

Times of Adversity 109

Worry. 111

V. My Home and Family

Godly Household. 116

For My Husband 118

Being a Godly Wife 120

Restoration for a Troubled Marriage 122

Becoming A Godly Women 124

For My Baby. 126

Being the Parent My Child Needs 129

Protection for My Children. 131

Correcting My Children 133

My Child's School & Teachers. 135

Future of My Children 137

My Child's Hunger for God 139

My Child's Spiritual Growth 141

Nighttime Prayer for My Children 143

For My Teenager 145

Teenager to Return to God 148

Observing Family Communion 151

Losing a Loved One. 153

VI. My Relationships

Walking in Love. 156

Communication With Others. 158

Forgiveness. 160

Favor. 162

Choosing the Right Friends 164

For Another's Salvation 166

Relationships 168

VII. Living My Life Everyday

Divine Protection 172

Safety for Travel 174

Staying Physically Fit 176

Healthy Eating Habits 178

Time Management 180

Finances 182

Giving 184

New Job 186

Being a Godly Employee 188

Finding the Right Church 190

Before a Church Service 192

VIII. Praying For Our Nation

The President 196

Congress 199

Military 202

Our Nation 204

National Patriotism 206

National Protection 208

Time of War 210

I

Growing In My Relationship With God

Start the Day Right

Lord, I thank You for the gift of this day. This is the day that You have made, and I will rejoice and be glad in it. I thank You, Lord, that Your mercy and grace are new every morning.

I rejoice because I am Your child. I have been filled with Your Spirit. Greater is He that is in me than he that is in the world. Holy Spirit, You are bigger than any problem, obstacle, calamity, or challenge that lies before me.

Lord, I thank You for the wonderful gift that You have provided in giving me this day. My gift back to You is what I do with this day for Your glory. Help me to honor You in all that I do today. I acknowledge You and lift You up today; therefore, You have promised to direct my steps, to order my life.

Let others see You in me today, and let my words minister grace to all those who hear them. Help me to be a blessing to the people around me. Help me to be a beacon of light, hope, and encouragement.

Lord, no matter what happens today, I trust You to see me through. I thank You that Your Word says that I can do all things through Christ who strengthens me and that if You be for me then no one can be against me. I thank You for Your favor in every area of my life today, in Jesus' name. Amen.

Scriptures

This is the day which the Lord hath made; we will rejoice and be glad in it (Psalm 118:24).

It is of the Lord's mercies that we are not consumed, because his compassions fail not. They are new every morning: great is thy faithfulness (Lamentations 3:22-23).

In all thy ways acknowledge him, and he shall direct thy paths (Proverbs 3:6).

Let no corrupt communication proceed out of your mouth, but that which is good to the use of edifying, that it may minister grace unto the hearers (Ephesians 4:29).

I can do all things through Christ which strengtheneth me (Philippians 4:13).

What shall we then say to these things? If God be for us, who can be against us? (Romans 8:31).

God is my Hope

Father God, in Jesus' name, I thank You that when I accepted the Lord Jesus as my personal Savior, Jesus Himself came to live in my heart. The Holy Spirit came to make His home in me. My life has been redeemed from destruction. My sins have been forgiven. I have been washed clean by the blood of my Lord and Savior, Jesus. My heart is new. Old things are passed way. The old person is dead, and I am a new woman. I became a new creature in Christ.

When I sin, I now have an advocate with the Father. When I ask for forgiveness, You are faithful and just to forgive me of my sins. When I need direction, the Holy Spirit is there to help me find my way. Your Word, Lord, is a lamp and a light in my life. Your Word is my standard to live by, my cornerstone for leading a life that is pleasing to You.

I have a new destiny for my life, a new hope, a new joy, and a new purpose. My eternal home is with my Lord and Savior. Forever I will be with You and all the saints in heaven. For eternity, I will praise Your name and enjoy Your presence.

Scriptures

Therefore if any man be in Christ, he is a new creature: old things are passed away; behold, all things are become new (2 Corinthians 5:17).

My little children, these things write I unto you, that ye sin not. And if any man sin, we have an advocate with the Father, Jesus Christ the righteous (1 John 2:1).

Thy word is a lamp unto my feet, and a light unto my path (Psalm 119:105).

God Loves Me This I Know

Father God, in Jesus' name, I thank You for Your bountiful love. Your love is so great that You spared not Your own Son but delivered Him up as a sacrifice that I might be reconciled to You. Your love is the greatest force in the world.

I thank You that nothing can separate me from Your love—not tribulation, distress, persecution, famine, peril, or battle. Your love, Lord, is the rock and foundation of my life. No matter what situation I face, no matter what challenges are before me, Your love shall sustain me.

I am more than a conqueror through Your love manifested in me. I know without a shadow of a doubt that nothing can separate me from Your love—not death, life, angels, principality, threats, things to come, powers, heights, or depths. Nothing in all creation can separate me from Your love, which is in Christ Jesus my Lord.

Scriptures

He that spared not his own Son, but delivered him up for us all, how shall he not with him also freely give us all things? (Romans 8:32).

Who shall separate us from the love of Christ? shall tribulation, or distress, or persecution, or famine, or nakedness, or peril, or sword? (Romans 8:35).

Nay, in all these things we are more than conquerors through him that loved us (Romans 8:37).

The Greater One in Me

I thank You, Lord, that greater is He that is in me than he that is in the world. Lord, I thank You that You are greater than Satan and the forces of darkness. You are greater than sin, sickness, and disease. You are greater than lack, want, and need. You are greater than any circumstance I might face. You are greater than any obstacle that comes up before me. You are greater than any challenge that comes into my life. You are greater than any adversity that comes against me. Lord, You are greater than my own doubts, insecurities, or uncertainties. You are greater than anything this life can throw at me.

I am more than a conqueror through You, Lord. I can face the circumstances of life with boldness and confidence in You. You are greater, and You live in me. You put me over; You cause me to succeed; and with You, in Jesus' name, I cannot fail!

Scriptures

Ye are of God, little children, and have overcome them: because greater is he that is in you, than he that is in the world (1 John 4:4).

These things I have spoken unto you, that in me ye might have peace. In the world ye shall have tribulation: but be of good cheer; I have overcome the world (John 16:33).

Nay, in all these things we are more than conquerors through him that loved us (Romans 8:37).

The Gift of the Holy Spirit

Father God, I thank You for the gift of the Holy Spirit that You have given to me. I thank You that He is my comforter and counselor, my helper and intercessor. Holy Spirit, You are my advocate, my strengthener, and my partner in my walk of faith. You teach me all things. You will bring back to my remembrance the truths from Your Word.

Holy Spirit, I invite You into every aspect of my life. Show me God's ways. Help me to know my Father's will and to be a carrier of His loving kindness into my world today.

Give me wisdom and insight concerning every decision that I need to make. Anoint me that I might do my duties with excellence. Give me the strength and courage to do Your will and to be obedient to Your voice today. Quicken my mortal body that I might have the physical stamina, endurance, and strength to do all that is required of me.

Let the light of Your love shine brightly through me today. Holy Spirit, live big and bold in me today. Help me to apply the truth and principles of God's Word to every area of my life. In Jesus' name I pray. Amen.

Scriptures

And I will pray the Father, and he shall give you another Comforter, that he may abide with you for ever (John 14:16).

But the Comforter, which is the Holy Ghost, whom the Father will send in my name, he shall teach you all things, and bring all things to your remembrance, whatsoever I have said unto you (John 14:26).

But if the Spirit of him that raised up Jesus from the dead dwell in you, he that raised up Christ from the dead shall also quicken your mortal bodies by his Spirit that dwelleth in you (Romans 8:11).

My Strong Tower, My Refuge

I thank You, Lord, that Your Word says that You are my refuge and strong tower. You are my fortress and place of security and safety. Help me to live in that place of confidence and peace.

Because I have made You, Lord, my refuge and my dwelling place, no evil shall befall me; no plague or calamity shall come near my home or my family. You give Your angels charge over me to accompany, defend, and preserve me in all my ways. Wherever I go and whatever I do, Your angels go with me to protect me from harm, injury, and evil.

Even though I may walk in the midst of danger and peril, it will have no effect on me. Because You have set Your love on me, You will deliver me and set me on high. Because I have made You my refuge, Your mercy, grace, and kindness surround me like a cloud. I will call upon You, and You will answer me. You will be with me in times of trouble, and You will deliver me and honor me. With a long life, You satisfy me and show me Your salvation.

In that place of refuge, I receive Your wisdom and insight. In that place of refuge, I hear Your voice clearly and receive direction and guidance for every area of my life. Thank You for being my refuge, in Jesus' name. Amen.

Scriptures

The name of the Lord is a strong tower; the righteous run to it and are safe (Proverbs 18:10 NIV).

There shall no evil befall thee, neither shall any plague come nigh thy dwelling, for he shall give his angels charge over thee, to keep thee in all thy ways (Psalm 91:10-11).

With long life will I satisfy him and show him my salvation (Psalm 91:16 NIV).

Teach me to do your will, for you are my God; may your good Spirit lead me on level ground (Psalm 143:10 NIV).

Dwelling in the Secret Place

Lord, help me to enter into the place of Your presence. Help me to enter into that place of rest and peace that can only be found in Your presence.

Lord, I thank You in Jesus' name that I have chosen to dwell in Your secret place, and because I have done so, I remain stable and fixed under Your shadow. You are my refuge and my fortress, my God. I lean and rely on You, and I confidently place my trust in You. I thank You that You deliver me from the snare of the fowler and from the deadly pestilence. I thank You that You cover me with Your wings of protection, and under those wings I find a safe haven. Your truth and Your faithfulness are my shield and buckler.

Because of Your divine protection in my life, I am not afraid of the terror at night or the evil plots and slanders of the wicked that fly by day. I am not afraid of the pestilence that stalks in darkness. I am not afraid of the destruction, calamity, or sudden death with which the enemy would try to attack me.

A thousand may fall at my side and ten thousand at my right hand, but it shall not, will not, and cannot come near me or my family, because we are inaccessible in the secret place of the Most High.

Scriptures

He that dwelleth in the secret place of the most High shall abide under the shadow of the Almighty (Psalm 91:1).

And they that know thy name will put their trust in thee: for thou, Lord, hast not forsaken them that seek thee (Psalm 9:10).

A thousand may fall at your side, ten thousand at your right hand, but it will not come near you (Psalm 91:7 NIV*).*

God Complete Your Work in Me

You, Lord, light my way before me. You give me clear instruction and keep me firmly on the paths of righteousness. I claim victory over the enemy. I can run through a garrison and leap over fortified walls. Your Word is ever before me. It is tested, tried, and true. I put my complete trust in You. You are my shield and my refuge. You are my rock and my fortress. You are my hiding place and strong tower. You enlighten me with Your understanding concerning the plan You have for my life. You have set me free from all hindrances. You have made my feet like those of a deer, firm and able, swift and graceful. You have made me secure and capable in You. I maintain a steadfast resistance to the attacks of the enemy, and I live in a place of blessing and prominence because of Your love for me.

Your Spirit leads and directs my steps. He is my helper and my friend. He gives me wisdom, insight, and clarity concerning the decisions I make. Your wisdom and counsel establish the firm foundation of my faith. By Your Word, Your precepts and principles are established in my heart and bring strength and stability to my life.

Lord, work in me and through me to fulfill Your plan and purpose for my life. Use me to minister Your love to those whose lives I touch. As I acknowledge and worship You, I thank You that You direct and guide my steps. In Jesus' name I pray. Amen.

Scriptures

He restoreth my soul: he leadeth me in the paths of righteousness for his name's sake (Psalm 23:3).

The Lord is my rock, and my fortress, and my deliverer; my God, my strength, in whom I will trust; my buckler, and the horn of my salvation, and my high tower (Psalm 18:2).

He maketh my feet like hinds' feet: and setteth me upon my high places (2 Samuel 22:34).

Likewise the Spirit also helpeth our infirmities: for we know not what we should pray for as we ought: but the Spirit itself maketh intercession for us with groanings which cannot be uttered (Romans 8:26).

Prayer of Contentment

Lord help me to be content with my life. Help me to realize my life is a work in progress and I will never achieve perfection. Reveal the secret to me on how to reach for excellence with out demanding perfection from myself or others.

Show me how to strive for success but maintain contentment. How to work hard to achieve my goals without their achievement being my only aim. Reveal to me how to enjoy the rewards of my labor but to never become materialistic. Let me rejoice when others succeed and not become jealous or envious of their accomplishments. Help how to be satisfied with out being complacent. Help me to be at peace but not be passive. Help me to enjoy where I am at on the way to where I want to go, Create within me a grateful spirit and thankful heart. In all my relationships with others help me to expect nothing but appreciate everything. Help me to maintain spirit gratitude in all things and all times realizing there are multitudes less fortunate than I. Let Your peace that passes all understanding guide and govern all my decisions.

Scriptures

Let your conversation be without covetousness; and be content with such things as ye have: for he hath said, I will never leave thee, nor forsake thee (Hebrews 13:5).

But the Comforter, which is the Holy Ghost, whom the Father will send in my name, he shall teach you all things, and bring all things to your remembrance, whatsoever I have said unto you (John 14:26).

I know what it is to be in need, and I know what it is to have plenty. I have learned the secret of being content in any and every situation, whether well fed or hungry, whether living in plenty or in want (Philippians 4:12 NIV).

Do not be anxious about anything, but in everything, by prayer and petition, with thanksgiving, present your requests to God (Philippians 4:6 NIV).

Being Thankful

Thank You, Lord, for caring for me and loving me even when I am unlovely. Thank You for dying for me and providing salvation for me.

Thank You for the gift of the Holy Spirit and for the gift of Your Word. I know that Your Word and the Holy Spirit will lead and guide me.

I know, Lord, that Your mercies are new every morning. Thank You for Your inexhaustible supply of forgiveness and love. You, Lord, encourage me when I am down and believe in me when I doubt myself. I thank You for lifting me up when I am discouraged and for giving me Your peace.

You are truly a friend who sticks closer than a brother. You are always there to take care of my every need. Help me to remember to always have a thankful heart and an attitude of gratitude. Help me to never take for granted all that You have done for me. In Jesus' name I pray. Amen.

Scriptures

His compassions fail not. They are new every morning: great is thy faithfulness (Lamentations 3:22-23).

Peace I leave with you, my peace I give unto you: not as the world giveth, give I unto you. Let not your heart be troubled, neither let it be afraid (John 14:27).

A man that hath friends must show himself friendly: and there is a friend that sticketh closer than a brother (Proverbs 18:24).

O give thanks unto the Lord; for he is good; for his mercy endureth for ever (1 Chronicles 16:34).

Praise and Worship

Father, in Jesus' name, I come to You to praise and worship You and to lift You up. I lift up Your name and exalt You. In all things I praise You—even when I am tempted to worry, even in the midst of the battle. I worship You. I acknowledge You, Lord. I put You first in my life. You are worthy to be praised. You are my rock and my fortress, my strong tower. You are my shield and ever-present help in my time of need. You are my hiding place.

There is power in praising You. Worship gives me strength to endure, to overcome. Worship fills me with Your presence. Worship gives me hope and makes me alive unto You. Worship gives me spiritual strength to continue. As I acknowledge You, I thank You that according to Your Word You direct my paths. I honor You, and You bring honor to my life.

I present myself before You as a living sacrifice to be used of You, Lord. Let Your love, grace, and mercy flow from my heart, I pray. I will praise You because You are a good God and You love me. Your love encompasses me. I praise You because You are with me, for me, and in me. I give You worship, praise, and thanksgiving. Because You are for me, no one can be against me. I shall not fear or have any anxiety or stress, but I put my trust and confidence in You.

Praising You, Lord, gives me strength, peace, and fulfillment.

Scriptures

And he said, The Lord is my rock, and my fortress, and my deliverer (2 Samuel 22:2).

Let us therefore come boldly unto the throne of grace, that we may obtain mercy, and find grace to help in time of need (Hebrews 4:16).

Thy word is a lamp unto my feet, and a light unto my path (Psalm 119:105).

I beseech you therefore, brethren, by the mercies of God, that ye present your bodies a living sacrifice, holy, acceptable unto God, which is your reasonable service (Romans 12:1).

What shall we then say to these things? If God be for us, who can be against us? (Romans 8:31).

Loving Myself as God Loves Me

Heavenly Father, I ask that You help me to love myself. Help me to see myself the way You see me, as a valuable gift for whose redemption You gave the life of Your own Son. Help me to realize that You have placed within me unique qualities, talents, and gifts. Help me to appreciate what You have done for me.

Help me to see with Your eyes, not with my eyes or others' eyes. Help me to recognize that I am a work in progress and that, even though I am not what I want to be, I am not what I used to be. I am growing in You and am beautiful in Your sight.

Give me confidence to love myself the way You love me. Help me to not be critical or condemning of myself but to encourage myself in You. Help me to be quick to forgive myself when I make mistakes and quick to encourage myself. Help me to realize that, even with all my shortcomings, You love me and believe in me. Help me to do the same for myself.

I recognize that it is Your will that I let Your light and love shine through me to my husband, children, friends, and all those I meet. I also realize that if I do not love myself, then it is hard for me to love others. Help me to not listen to the voice of the enemy or to the voice of others, but to listen to Your voice. Your Word says that I am unique, that I am a special gift, that I am a treasure in Your sight. I choose to believe You and to order my life by that. Give me confidence and faith to love myself, in Jesus' name. Amen.

Scriptures

But God, who is rich in mercy, for his great love wherewith he loved us, even when we were dead in sins, hath quickened us together with Christ, (by grace ye are saved;) and hath raised us up together, and made us sit together in heavenly places in Christ Jesus (Ephesians 2:4-6).

Wherefore comfort yourselves together, and edify one another, even as also ye do (1 Thessalonians 5:11).

I will praise thee; for I am fearfully and wonderfully made: marvellous are thy works; and that my soul knoweth right well (Psalm 139:14).

End the Day Strong

Lord, as I come to You at the end of this day, I thank You for being faithful to me and to my family. Thank You for providing for us. Thank You for sustaining us and protecting us. Thank You for Your blessings in every area of our lives.

Holy Spirit, reveal to me anything that I may have said or done that was displeasing to You, so that I can repent for it, receive Your forgiveness, and go and sin no more. If I caused harm or injury to anyone, I ask You to forgive me and to heal their hurts.

Now help me to not worry or have any frustration or anxiety about any mistakes I made today. I cast all the cares and concerns of today's events upon You. I forget the past and look toward tomorrow. Lord, I thank You for the peace that resides in my heart, in my life, and in my home. Thank You, Lord, that tomorrow is a new day. I thank You that no matter how many times I stumbled today I can start fresh and new in You tomorrow.

I trust You to fulfill Your plans and purposes in me and my family. Lord, I thank You that You are designing my future before me. I thank You for a restful night's sleep, in Jesus' name. Amen.

Scriptures

Casting all your care upon him; for he careth for you (1 Peter 5:7).

It is of the Lord's mercies that we are not consumed, because his compassions fail not. They are new every morning: great is thy faithfulness (Lamentations 3:22-23).

I will lie down and sleep in peace, for you alone, O Lord, make me dwell in safety (Psalm 4:8 NIV).

II

Growing In God

Growing Up Spiritually

Lord, help me to grow spiritually. Help me to not let the daily activities and responsibilities of being a mother fill my life to the point that I have no time for prayer, worship, and devotional times with You.

Holy Spirit, please prompt me to spend time with You, and help me to remember to put You first and to block out time every day to invest in my spiritual growth. Help me to set priorities and to recognize time stealers. Give me the strength to say no before I overcommit or take on more than I can handle.

Lord, increase my desire for spiritual things. Reveal to me areas where I need to grow. Help me to be conscious of everyday opportunities to pray, to meditate on Your Word, to speak Your Word, and to apply Your Word to my life. I humble myself before You. Teach me Your ways, direct my steps, let Your Word become alive in me. Help me to always be sensitive to what You want to do in my life. In Jesus' name I pray. Amen.

Scriptures

Teach me to do thy will; for thou art my God: thy spirit is good; lead me into the land of uprightness (Psalm 143:10).

For the fruit of the Spirit is in all goodness and righteousness and truth (Ephesians 5:9).

Show me thy ways, O Lord; teach me thy paths (Psalm 25:4).

Craving God

Lord, in Jesus' name I pray that You would create a deeper hunger in my heart for You. Restore to my life the desire, passion, and thirst for You that I had when I first became a Christian. Lord, I love You, but I want to have a hunger for You. Help me to fall in love with You again. Let my main goal in life be to know You and the depths of Your love and compassion.

Unveil Yourself and reveal Your character to me. Help me to become passionately and deeply acquainted with You. I crave Your presence in and on my life throughout the day. I want to know You better.

Help me to be sensitive to the voice of Your Spirit. Let me see with Your eyes and hear with Your ears. Let me be a carrier of Your love and compassion to the world.

I pray, Lord, that Your presence will become such an intimate part of my life that others will see You in every part of my character. Fill my life to overflowing with Your presence. I pray that knowing You intimately will become the greatest quest of my life.

Scriptures

As the hart panteth after the water brooks, so panteth my soul after thee, O God (Psalm 42:1).

That Christ may dwell in your hearts by faith; that ye, being rooted and grounded in love, may be able to comprehend with all saints what is the breadth, and length, and depth, and height (Ephesians 3:17-18).

And be not drunk with wine, wherein is excess; but be filled with the Spirit (Ephesians 5:18).

A Women of Faithfulness

Father, in the name of Jesus, I ask You to help me be faithful in every area of my life. Your Word says that the faithful shall abound in blessings. Help me to be consistent to put off discouragement. Help me to be faithful at church, to be a good example, to be a hard worker, and to not get my feelings hurt when things happen that I don't understand. When I am tempted to be offended because of what others say or do, Lord, let it not affect my faithfulness.

Help me to be faithful in my prayer life, faithful in my commitment to You, faithful to my friends, and faithful to my children. I commit to pray for them and be an encouragement to them. Let my children and those who are close to me see the quality of faithfulness in every area of my life—as a woman, as a wife, as a mother, as a friend, and as a church member.

Help me to be faithful, considerate, helpful, and supportive to those whom my life influences. Thank You, Lord, that the characteristic of faithfulness is a growing and maturing fruit in my life. But most of all, Lord, help me to be faithful to You. Help me to live my life so that at the end of my days, I will be ushered into Your presence with the words "Welcome, thou good and faithful servant."

Help me to be a dependable person—one who honors and keeps her word. Help me to use discretion and confidentiality when dealing with sensitive issues and to be faithful to the trust that others have given me. Help me to have dedicated loyalty to those for whom I work, to my family and friends, and to my church. In Jesus' name I pray. Amen.

Scriptures

A faithful man shall abound with blessings. (Proverbs 28:20).

But the fruit of the Spirit is love, joy, peace, longsuffering, gentleness, goodness, faith, meekness, temperance: against such there is no law (Galatians 5:22-23).

His lord said unto him, Well done, good and faithful servant; thou hast been faithful over a few things, I will make thee ruler over many things: enter thou into the joy of thy lord (Matthew 25:23).

A Fervent Women of Prayer

Father, You said that through prayer and supplication I should let my requests be made known to You. You said to come boldly to Your throne room to receive grace and mercy. Your Word says that whatsoever things I desire when I pray, when I believe that I receive them, I shall have them. I desire to be a person of prayer.

Help me to not let the busyness of life rob me from the joy, privilege, and power of spending time with You in prayer. Put a desire in my heart to pray more and to make prayer a prominent part of my life. Help me to establish certain times of the day to pray and seek Your wisdom. Help me not to be distracted during my prayer time, but to be able to focus my thoughts, my heart, and my faith on You and Your Word.

Use me, Lord, to pray for others. Help me to be sensitive to the voice of the Holy Spirit. Help me to be quick to obey the call to prayer whenever I sense Your direction to pray. Let prayer become so significant to me that it becomes my natural response to every situation in life.

Your Word says that the effectual, fervent prayer of the righteous avails much. Teach me to pray effectively. Show me how to pray with passion and fervor, so that my prayers do avail much. In Jesus' name I pray. Amen.

Scriptures

Be careful for nothing; but in every thing by prayer and supplication with thanksgiving let your requests be made known unto God (Philippians 4:6).

Let us therefore come boldly unto the throne of grace, that we may obtain mercy, and find grace to help in time of need (Hebrews 4:16).

Therefore I say unto you, What things soever ye desire, when ye pray, believe that ye receive them, and ye shall have them (Mark 11:24).

Likewise the Spirit also helpeth our infirmities: for we know not what we should pray for as we ought: but the Spirit itself maketh intercession for us with groanings which cannot be uttered (Romans 8:26).

The effectual fervent prayer of a righteous man availeth much (James 5:16).

I Can Be the Woman God Says I Am

Lord, help me to glorify You in my role as a woman. I desire to lead a godly life and to be an example of the Christian walk. Help me to have balance in my life, properly spending time with You, Lord, and time with family and friends.

Help me to be sensitive to the needs of my friends and to be understanding of their feelings. I ask You for Your wisdom and discernment concerning all my decisions. When I make a mistake, help me to be quick to ask for forgiveness.

Let me be an example of what to do when things go wrong, as well as when they go right. Help me to keep my cool and not become frustrated and lose my temper. If I do something that is wrong or offensive, let me be quick to repent. Help me to be peaceful, consistent, and faithful. Help me to walk in love at all times and to be quick to provide encouragement and inspiration to those with whom I speak.

Help me to recognize the gifts and talents that You have placed in me. Help me to cultivate and develop these gifts for Your glory, O Lord. I pray that people will see You in me in every area of my life. In Jesus' name I pray. Amen.

Scriptures

We should live soberly, righteously, and godly, in this present world (Titus 2:12).

If any of you lack wisdom, let him ask of God, that giveth to all men liberally, and upbraideth not; and it shall be given him (James 1:5).

Be thou an example of the believers, in word, in conversation, in charity, in spirit, in faith, in purity (1 Timothy 4:12).

A Proverbs Woman

Lord, help me to develop the qualities and characteristics of the Proverbs 31 woman. Let me be a capable, intelligent, and virtuous woman, more precious than jewels. Let my value to my family be far above that of rubies or pearls.

Help me be the kind of woman whom my husband can trust and believe in securely. Lord, let my husband know his heart and dreams are safe with me. Help me to comfort him, encourage him, and do him only good.

Help me, Lord, to provide all the things my family needs—food, clothing, and a clean house. Let me do my tasks without complaining or despairing.

Father, help me to be wise in my spending habits. Help me to not be impulsive or irresponsible, but to use wisdom and discretion in every purchase.

Lord, help me to look my best for my husband and family. Let me be clothed on the outside with fine clothing and clothed with Your Word on the inside.

May I be an inspiration and encouragement to those around me. Help me to speak words of life, help, and hope and never words of criticism, gossip, or discouragement.

Lord, let my children see You in me. Help me to show them how to walk in Your paths.

Lord, help me to live my life in such a way that I bring honor to You and to my family. Help me to be all that I can be in You. Let me be a virtuous woman. In Jesus' name I pray. Amen.

Scriptures

Who can find a virtuous woman? for her price is far above rubies (Proverbs 31:10).

She openeth her mouth with wisdom; and in her tongue is the law of kindness (Proverbs 31:26).

Her children arise up, and call her blessed; her husband also, and he praiseth her (Proverbs 31:28).

Being Comfortable with My Body

Heavenly Father, help me to be comfortable with my body and to not be concerned with all the imperfection I see in myself. When I look in the mirror I see so many things I would like to be different or change. Let me see myself the way You see me, Your word says I am beautiful in Your site. The world sees beauty on the outside but You see beauty in what we are in our heart, in our thoughts, our words and our actions. Your word says my body is a temple of the Holy Spirit, a vessel for You to use in this world. Fill my mouth with encouraging words, fill my heart with love for others and show me how to make a difference in my actions toward others.

Whether I am fat or thin, short or tall, young or old, my body is beautiful in Your eyes. Show me Lord, how to stop comparing myself with others who seem to be more appealing and start comparing myself with what and who the Bible says I am. I am unquiely and wonderfully made, I have Your mind and Your peace in my life. When thoughts come of inadequacy in my body, let me replace them with words of strength and courage. Reveal to me ways to help others see themselves as beautiful in Your site. As I encourage others I pray I will be encouraged as well.

Lord, I pray for strength to face all the imperfection I see and call them wonderful, because You have made me in Your image. I am a exact copy of You and You are beautiful, You are all that I want to be. Thank you Lord, for creating my and making me the way I am.

Scriptures

What? know ye not that your body is the temple of the Holy Ghost which is in you, which ye have of God, and ye are not your own? (1 Corinthians 6:19).

Who satisfieth thy mouth with good things; so that thy youth is renewed like the eagle's (Psalm 103:5).

I will praise thee; for I am fearfully and wonderfully made: marvellous are thy works; and that my soul knoweth right well (Psalm 139:14).

I beseech you therefore, brethren, by the mercies of God, that ye present your bodies a living sacrifice, holy, acceptable unto God, which is your reasonable service (Romans 12:1).

Balance In My Life

Lord I need balance in my life, it seems that the busyness of life keeps me off balance. There is always more to do than I can possibly get done. The urgent things are constantly at war with the important things in my life.

Sometimes frustration and guilt rob me of my joy. The amount of work, the responsibilities of life, the mile long to do list, keep yelling at me go faster, go faster. Sometimes I feel like I am on a never ending treadmill. Show me how I can be more effective, more balanced, and keep my joy and peace in the midst of a whirlwind of activity.

Help me to realize there is much more to life than increasing it's speed. Show me how to focus more on quality instead of just quantity. Help me to put my priorities in perspective. Help me to find a rhythm for my life. Reveal to me how I can incorporate the balance between work and rest, worship and play. Balance my busyness with solitude, my work with rest. Let me walk away from time to time so I can return refreshed and renewed.

Scriptures

Fear thou not; for I am with thee: be not dismayed; for I am thy God: I will strengthen thee; yea, I will help thee; yea, I will uphold thee with the right hand of my righteousness (Isaiah 41:10).

Casting all your care upon him: for he careth for you (1 Peter 5:7)

Do not be anxious about anything, but in everything by prayer and petition, with thanksgiving, present your requests to God (Philippians 4:6)

And the peace of God, which transcends all understanding, will guard your hearts and your minds in Christ Jesus (Philippians 4:7)

Fear thou not; for I am with thee: be not dismayed; for I am thy God: I will strengthen thee

Refreshing My Mind with God's Word

Dear heavenly Father, in Jesus' name, I dedicate myself to renewing my mind by reading, meditating, and speaking Your Word. Lord, it is my desire to keep my mind pure and clear from anything that would hurt me or damage my relationship with You. Your Word says to think on things that are pure, lovely, just, of a good report, and of virtue and praise.

You said in Your Word to take every thought captive. I choose to think about good things, and I refuse thoughts that are inappropriate for Your children. Lord, when I am tempted to doubt, worry, or fear, help me to speak Your promises, to overcome the attacks on my mind with answers from Your Word. Lord, let me be quick to respond to wrong thoughts and desires by replacing them with proper thoughts.

I refuse to fill my mind with the poison of gossip, backbiting, and jealousy. I make a quality decision to meditate on Your Word and to keep my mind pure and honest that I might be receptive to Your voice and ever ready to do Your will. Lord, I know that with Your help, I can win the battle in my mind and overcome every wrong thought with the power of the spoken Word.

I choose to consecrate my mind, my will, and my emotions to You, Lord, for Your service. In Jesus' name I pray. Amen.

Scriptures

And be not conformed to this world: but be ye transformed by the renewing of your mind, that ye may prove what is that good, and acceptable, and perfect, will of God (Romans 12:2).

Finally, brethren, whatsoever things are true, whatsoever things are honest, whatsoever things are just, whatsoever things are pure, whatsoever things are lovely, whatsoever things are of good report; if there be any virtue, and if there be any praise, think on these things (Philippians 4:8).

Casting down imaginations, and every high thing that exalteth itself against the knowledge of God, and bringing into captivity every thought to the obedience of Christ (2 Corinthians 10:5).

Saying God's Words

Dear Father, in Jesus' name, I pray that You would help me to be mindful of the words I speak as I go about my day. Your Word says that by my words I am justified and by my words I am condemned. Help me to put a guard over my mouth. If I say something that I should not, please bring it to my attention so I may correct it.

I choose to walk in love and not react in anger. Help me to think before I speak words that I would later regret. I choose to not gossip, criticize, condemn, or complain but only to speak words that encourage, uplift, and inspire others.

I understand that my words affect those who hear them. Help me to be thoughtful to choose the right words to express myself so that I may clearly communicate with others in a positive, inoffensive way.

I put Your Word in my mouth, and I speak Your promises over my life and the lives of others throughout the day. Speak through me today. Let Your words be my words. Help me to be sensitive to the needs of others, to be quick to speak words of comfort, peace, and kindness to them. May my words minister grace and mercy to all who hear them. Let me speak words that bring honor and glory to Your name.

Scriptures

For by thy words thou shalt be justified, and by thy words thou shalt be condemned (Matthew 12:37).

Put on therefore, as the elect of God, holy and beloved, bowels of mercies, kindness, humbleness of mind, meekness, longsuffering; forbearing one another, and forgiving one another, if any man have a quarrel against any: even as Christ forgave you, so also do ye. And above all these things put on charity, which is the bond of perfectness (Colossians 3:12-14).

Let no corrupt communication proceed out of your mouth, but that which is good to the use of edifying, that it may minister grace unto the hearers (Ephesians 4:29).

Finding My Purpose In Life

Lord I ask you to help me to discover and to fulfill your plan and purpose for my life. I bring all my desires, goals, and aspirations to you Lord. Reveal to me if they need to be adjusted, modified, or eliminated from my life. Help to discern what your perfect will is for my life. The cry of my heart is sincerely Lord not my will but your will concerning every aspect of my life. Create within me a willing and obedient heart. I will say what you tell me to say. I will do what you ask me to do. I will go where you ask me to go.

Help me to get on track, stay on track, and see to the end the plans and purposes you have destined for my life. Bring into my life the right people at the right time to partner with me so that I might accomplish all that you have called me to do. I thank you for your favor that goes before me to prepare my way, to open doors of opportunity to create the right conditions, the right alliances, the right tools, the right environment that I might fulfill your purpose in my life.

Scriptures

That Christ may dwell in your hearts by faith; that ye, being rooted and grounded in love, may be able to comprehend with all saints what is the breadth, and length, and depth, and height (Ephesians 3:17-18).

For I know the thoughts that I think toward you, saith the Lord, thoughts of peace, and not of evil, to give you an expected end (Jeremiah 29:11).

The eyes of your understanding being enlightened; that ye may know what is the hope of his calling, and what the riches of the glory of his inheritance in the saints (Ephesians 1:18).

I will instruct thee and teach thee in the way which thou shalt go: I will guide thee with mine eye (Psalm 32:8).

Lord Show Yourself Strong

Dear Father God, in Jesus' name, I proclaim that I am strong in You. I am empowered through my union with You. I draw strength from You for every battle that I face. I put on Your whole armor today, and in doing so I put myself in a position to successfully stand against all the strategies, deceits, and attacks of Satan and the forces of darkness.

I recognize that I wrestle not against flesh and blood, that humans are not my enemy. I will not direct my attack toward any person. My opponents are principalities, powers, and the rulers of the darkness of this world. Satan is a defeated foe, and he is under my feet. I resist him steadfast in faith, and he runs in terror when I speak Your Word.

Because of Your armor, Lord, I am able to resist every attack, stand my ground, and be victorious in the day of conflict. When crisis comes to my life, I am bold to fight and to proclaim Your Word. Standing upon Your promises in the midst of the battle, I know that ultimate victory is certain in You.

Lord, I thank You that You cause me to triumph in every situation through Christ Jesus my Savior.

Scriptures

Put on the whole armour of God, that ye may be able to stand against the wiles of the devil (Ephesians 6:11).

For we wrestle not against flesh and blood, but against principalities, against powers, against the rulers of the darkness of this world, against spiritual wickedness in high places (Ephesians 6:12).

Submit yourselves therefore to God. Resist the devil, and he will flee from you (James 4:7).

Now thanks be unto God, which always causeth us to triumph in Christ, and maketh manifest the savour of his knowledge by us in every place (2 Corinthians 2:14).

Having a Character Like God

Father, I present myself as a living sacrifice before You. You said that my life brings glory to You when I bear much fruit.

Help me to be fruitful in every area of my life. Help me to develop the fruit of the Spirit in my life: love, joy, peace, longsuffering, gentleness, goodness, faithfulness, meekness, and self-control.

I want to be a good representative of You, Lord. I pray that others would see You in me. Let the fruit of Your Spirit be the dominating characteristics of my life.

Let me be more considerate of others than I am of myself. Help me to be focused on bearing fruit and ministering to others instead of acting selfishly and demanding my own way.

You said in Your Word that You have chosen me and ordained me that I should go and bring forth fruit in my life. Thank You for helping me to do so, in Jesus' name. Amen.

Scriptures

I beseech you therefore, brethren, by the mercies of God, that ye present your bodies a living sacrifice, holy, acceptable unto God, which is your reasonable service (Romans 12:1).

But the fruit of the Spirit is love, joy, peace, longsuffering, gentleness, goodness, faith, meekness, temperance: against such there is no law (Galatians 5:22-23).

Ye have not chosen me, but I have chosen you, and ordained you, that ye should go and bring forth fruit, and that your fruit should remain: that whatsoever ye shall ask of the Father in my name, he may give it you (John 15:16).

Rejoicing in the Lord

I thank You, Lord, that this is the day that You have made. I will rejoice and be glad in it. I rejoice because once I was lost, but now I am found. Once I was blind, but now I see. Once I was on my way to hell, but now I am on my way to heaven.

Lord, I will rejoice because Your love has redeemed me from destruction and has filled me with Your righteousness. I can rejoice today because You promised to never leave me or forsake me.

Help me to rejoice in the midst of trials and tribulation. Help me to keep my mind focused on You and Your Word even in the middle of adversity and conflict. Help me to realize that my joy is not based on the circumstances around me but is the result of Your presence within me. Therefore, I can rejoice and shout for joy. Because You love me, Your desire is for me to be blessed and fulfilled in every area of my life. You are a great and wonderful God, and I will rejoice in Your name forever. In Jesus' name I pray. Amen.

Scriptures

I will be glad and rejoice in thee: I will sing praise to thy name, O thou most High (Psalm 9:2).

Let the redeemed of the Lord say so, whom he hath redeemed from the hand of the enemy (Psalm 107:2).

Then he said unto them, Go your way, eat the fat, and drink the sweet, and send portions unto them for whom nothing is prepared: for this day is holy unto our Lord: neither be ye sorry; for the joy of the Lord is your strength (Nehemiah 8:10).

III

When You Need...

When You Need...Confidence

Father, in Jesus' name I ask You to help me to be bold and confident. Let me not look at my failures and weaknesses but consider Your strength and abilities that You have promised to give me.

Lord, You told me in Your Word to love others as I love myself. Help me to love myself and to have a good self-image. Help me to not be judgmental or condemning of myself but to love myself as You love me. Let me forgive myself just as You have forgiven me. Let me not be critical and uptight about my shortcomings, but help me to realize that I am not perfect and never will be while I live in the earth. Help me to realize that living a Christian life is a journey and not a destination.

You said in Your Word that greater is He that is in me than he that is in the world. Your Word says that I can be more than a conqueror through Christ Jesus. I can do all things through Christ who strengthens me. You said, Lord, that the same Spirit that raised Jesus from the dead lives in me.

Father, I am bold to proclaim that I am confident because of Your work in me. I can operate in confidence in every area of my life, not because of who I am but because of who You are in me.

Thank You, Lord, for continuing that good work which You started in me. Let Your Word bring confidence and completion in my life in Jesus' name. Amen.

Scriptures

And he answering said, Thou shalt love the Lord thy God with all thy heart, and with all thy soul, and with all thy strength, and with all thy mind; and thy neighbour as thyself (Luke 10:27).

Ye are of God, little children, and have overcome them: because greater is he that is in you, than he that is in the world (1 John 4:4).

Nay, in all these things we are more than conquerors through him that loved us (Romans 8:37).

I can do all things through Christ which strengtheneth me (Philippians 4:13).

Being confident of this very thing, that he which hath begun a good work in you will perform it until the day of Jesus Christ (Philippians 1:6).

When You Need...Courage

I will be strong and courageous in You, O Lord. I have complete confidence in Your ability to give me the victory. I encounter every danger and difficulty with firmness and without fear. I am brave, bold, and resolute. I fulfill my calling in a spirit of valor and determination that overcomes any obstacle that the enemy would put in my path.

I do not turn from Your Word, Lord. I make it the cornerstone of my life so that I may prosper in all that I do. I speak Your Word continually. I meditate upon Your Word day and night so that I may do all that is written within it. By doing this I make my way prosperous, have good success, and deal wisely in all the affairs of my life. I give Your Word first place, O Lord. In my life, I make Your Word the final authority. I am faithful, strong, vigorous, bold, and very courageous. Fear has no place in me, for You are with me wherever I go and whatever I do.

I am as bold as a lion because of my union with You. I am not afraid to do what is right. I am not afraid of the future, because I know You will never leave me or forsake me. By the power of Your Spirit in me, I can face the uncertainties of life with an undaunted spirit of courage and confidence. In Jesus' name I proclaim it. Amen.

Scriptures

> *For whatsoever is born of God overcometh the world: and this is the victory that overcometh the world, even our faith (1 John 5:4).*
>
> *This book of the law shall not depart out of thy mouth; but thou shalt meditate therein day and night, that thou mayest observe to do according to all that is written therein: for then thou shalt make thy way prosperous, and then thou shalt have good success (Joshua 1:8).*
>
> *For he hath said, I will never leave thee, nor forsake thee (Hebrews 13:5).*

When You Need...Discernment

Lord, in Jesus' name, I ask You for discernment. Give me wisdom and insight concerning all the matters in my life. Help me to be sensitive to Your voice. Give me direction and guidance concerning every decision that I am faced with today. Help me to have a discerning heart and mind when I deal with people and issues that must be confronted. Bring clarity to my heart and mind regarding any situation that requires my attention, and help me to respond with the appropriate action.

Help me to be solution-minded and to be considerate of others as I make decisions today. Allow me to see with Your eyes and hear with Your ears and operate in Your wisdom so that I make the right choices in my life. Help me to make decisions objectively and not emotionally. Help me to determine Your will and desire concerning every area of my life.

As a mother, I desire Your wisdom to discern what is the proper way to handle the conflicts that arise within and between my children and to bring a quick and accurate solution. As I acknowledge and worship You, I thank You that You direct my steps and order my life by Your Spirit.

Scriptures

If any of you lack wisdom, let him ask of God, that giveth to all men liberally, and upbraideth not; and it shall be given him (James 1:5).

The steps of a good man are ordered by the Lord: and he delighteth in his way (Psalm 37:23).

Order my steps in thy word: and let not any iniquity have dominion over me (Psalm 119:133).

When You Need...Faith

Lord, I thank You that You have given every believer a measure of faith. Lord, You are the author and finisher of my faith. You bring to maturity and perfection the faith that You have placed within my heart.

You said that faith comes by hearing the Word of God. I make a conscious decision to read and meditate on Your Word every day, and as I do faith grows in my heart. You said that without faith it is impossible to please You. I want to please You: Help me to have strong faith. Faith is the assurance and confirmation, my title deed, of things that I hope for and the proof of things I do not see. I thank You, Lord, that the faith that is in my heart perceives the unseen promise as a real fact.

I am not moved by what I see but only by what I believe, and I believe You. By faith, I appropriate to my life every promise from Your Word. Regardless of the circumstances around me, Lord, I proclaim that Your promises are "yes and amen." Faith is alive and working in my life, and by faith I receive all that You have done for me, in Jesus' name. Amen.

Scriptures

God hath dealt to every man the measure of faith (Romans 12:3).

Looking unto Jesus the author and finisher of our faith; who for the joy that was set before him endured the cross, despising the shame, and is set down at the right hand of the throne of God (Hebrews 12:2).

So then faith cometh by hearing, and hearing by the word of God (Romans 10:17).

But without faith it is impossible to please him: for he that cometh to God must believe that he is, and that he is a rewarder of them that diligently seek him (Hebrews 11:6).

Now faith is the substance of things hoped for, the evidence of things not seen (Hebrews 11:1).

For all the promises of God in him are yea, and in him Amen, unto the glory of God by us (2 Corinthians 1:20).

When You Need...Guidance

Lord Jesus, I thank You that You have revealed to me through Your Word the secret of facing every situation. I know what to do when I find myself in adverse circumstances, and I know what to do when I am living in abundance: I thank You, Lord, that I have learned that in any and every circumstance You are my strength, my salvation, and my deliverer.

The power of Your Word in my life can redeem, rectify, and deliver me in every situation. I can do all things through Your power that is within me. Because of Your anointing and the power of Your Word, not a single circumstance can hold me down or stop me from living a life of victory. I am self-sufficient in Your sufficiency.

I thank You, Lord, that by the wisdom of Your Word and the guidance of Your Spirit I can navigate my way through any circumstance. Help me, Lord, to hear Your voice clearly and distinctly. Help me to be sensitive to the guidance of the Holy Spirit. Lord, let me rely completely on You and not on my own understanding. In Jesus' name I pray. Amen.

Scriptures

I know what it is to be in need, and I know what it is to have plenty. I have learned the secret of being content in any and every situation, whether well fed or hungry, whether living in plenty or in want (Philippians 4:12 NIV*).*

I can do all things through Christ which strengtheneth me (Philippians 4:13).

Trust in the Lord with all thine heart; and lean not unto thine own understanding (Proverbs 3:5).

When You Need...Healing

Dear heavenly Father, in Jesus' name, I come before You for healing in my body. I know that You are a good God, and You are a compassionate, loving Father who desires to see me healthy, whole, and free. I ask for Your healing power to touch my body right now. Help me to be strong in my faith and to receive Your healing for my body.

Jesus died on the cross for my salvation, but He also took stripes on His back for my healing; He bore my sickness and carried my diseases. The Bible says He Himself took our pains in His own body and that with His stripes we were healed.

As I read, study, and meditate on Your Scriptures about healing, I realize that the power of Your Word brings healing to my body. Let the truth of Your Word grow strong in my heart and bring healing to my body.

I receive the Scriptures regarding healing and make them my own. Jesus paid the price for my healing so that I am made whole. Now, Lord, I receive Your Word and believe it. I thank You and praise You for the healing that has begun in my body. Help me to see myself well and walking in health in Jesus' name.

Scriptures

But he was wounded for our transgressions, he was bruised for our iniquities: the chastisement of our peace was upon him; and with his stripes we are healed (Isaiah 53:5).

That it might be fulfilled which was spoken by Esaias the prophet, saying, Himself took our infirmities, and bare our sicknesses (Matthew 8:17).

He sent his word, and healed them, and delivered them from their destructions (Psalm 107:20).

When You Need...Integrity

Lord, in matters great and small, in all areas of my life, I pray that You would help me to live a life of integrity. Help me to never violate my conscience or my heart by justifying or excusing my actions that are not honorable before You. Help me remember that it is never right to do the wrong thing, no matter what the circumstances. Help me to never compromise my integrity for personal gain of any kind.

Let my word be my bond. Let me live my life with integrity and truth. Help me, Lord, to make integrity the foundation and cornerstone of my character. Let it never be said of me that I am dishonest or that I have operated or functioned in dishonesty or deception. Let integrity be the standard by which I govern my life. Let my choices be governed not by what is best for me, but only by what is the right thing to do. Then, Lord, give me courage and strength to always do that right thing.

Lord, I know that there will be times when I will be tempted by the enemy, by pride, or by selfishness to behave in such a manner that would compromise my integrity. Help me to always realize that anything for which I exchange my integrity costs too much, and nothing is worth that loss. In Jesus' name I pray. Amen.

Scriptures

> *Let integrity and uprightness preserve me; for I wait on thee (Psalm 25:21).*
>
> *And as for me, thou upholdest me in mine integrity, and settest me before thy face for ever (Psalm 41:12).*
>
> *The integrity of the upright shall guide them: but the perverseness of transgressors shall destroy them (Proverbs 11:3).*
>
> *The just man walketh in his integrity: his children are blessed after him (Proverbs 20:7).*

When You Need...Patience

Dear heavenly Father, I pray for patience in my life. Help me to trust You and to know that You have everything under control. Help me to stay steady and not overreact to people or situations but to be patient in all things. When life is hectic, demanding, and busy, help me to not let frustration and anxiety steal patience out of my heart.

Help me, Lord, to trust the work that You are doing in me. Help me to not strive for personal perfection but to allow You to be perfected in me. Lord, help me to run the race that is before me with patience, not to run too fast and not to make things happen in my future, but to let Your will be worked out in my life.

Help me to be patient in prayer. When it seems as if You are not answering my prayers as quickly as I desire, help me to patiently wait for Your deliverance. Instead of always wanting everything my way, let me be patient and see what You have for me.

Your Word says to let patience have her perfect work. Lord, let that perfect work begin in me. Help me to not be anxious, worried, or fretful, but to trust in, lean on, and rely upon You, knowing that You will work all things together for my good if I remain patient. Help me to realize that change and challenges are a normal part of life and to be patient during those times of tests and trials.

Lord, I pray for patience concerning my children and my husband. Let me see in them what You see in them. Help me to be a model of patience in my responses to them that I might see the manifestation of patience in their lives as well.

Let Your peace now guard over my heart and Your patience have its perfect work in me. In Jesus' name I pray. Amen.

Scriptures

But let patience have her perfect work, that ye may be perfect and entire, wanting nothing (James 1:4).

Trust in the Lord with all thine heart; and lean not unto thine own understanding (Proverbs 3:5).

And we know that all things work together for good to them that love God, to them who are the called according to his purpose (Romans 8:28).

And the peace of God, which passeth all understanding, shall keep your hearts and minds through Christ Jesus (Philippians 4:7).

When You Need...To Control My Emotions

Lord, show me how to get my emotions under control. I know that it's not Your will for me to be upset and out of control, I need to be at peace in my heart and mind. You created my emotions to have compassion and love for others, but not to let them rule over my life. When You walk on this earth You used Your emotions to minister to others and to help, let me do the same.

Help me to replace wrong emotions with Your word, if I am feeling sad, give me joy, if I am angered, give me peace and if I am lonely, fill me with Your love. Reveal to me the way to manage my emotions, to see them for what they are and why I am feeling the way I am. Lord, I know that You want the best for me, to be whole physically and emotionally. Let me use wrong emotions, anger, jealousy, envy, as stepping stones to love, acceptance, contentment. Lord, help me to take my wrong emotions and fear and replace them love and encouragement.

You are our example in this world, you where angry but didn't sin, you showed emotion but did not let it rule over you. You kept emotions in there place Lord, help me to do the same.

Scriptures

These things I have spoken unto you, that in me ye might have peace. In the world ye shall have tribulation: but be of good cheer; I have overcome the world (John 16:33).

His compassions fail not. They are new every morning: great is thy faithfulness (Lamentations 3:22-23).

And be not conformed to this world: but be ye transformed by the renewing of your mind, that ye may prove what is that good, and acceptable, and perfect, will of God (Romans 12:2).

For we wrestle not against flesh and blood, but against principalities, against powers, against the rulers of the darkness of this world, against spiritual wickedness in high places (Ephesians 6:12).

When You Need...To Simplify My Life

Lord, help me, I feel overwhelm! There are so many things I need to be doing and I don't seem to be getting any of them done. I need to simplify my life, but it seems that it gets more complicated. I know Your word says that I can do all things through Christ who stregenths me, help me to use that like a soldier uses a weapon.

Show me how to cast my cares and burdens on You because You care for me. Let me not compare myself with others who seem to "have it all together" but compare myself with what the Word says about me. I know I am in a battle for my peace and for my joy; the devil would love to take them away from me and leave me with fear and dread. Lord, I choose to believe Your word that says I am more than a conqueror; I am equal to any challenge that life can throw at me.

Show me Lord, how to make plans to simplify my life and effective ways to accomplice what needs to be done. Guide me in Your word to scriptures that will help me to put things in perspective. You are the ultimate planner, show me strategies to plan and then work my plan. Lord, thank you for helping me to simplify my life.

Scriptures

I can do all things through Christ which strengthen me (Philippians 4:13).

Who shall separate us from the love of Christ? shall tribulation, or distress, or persecution, or famine, or nakedness, or peril, or sword? Nay, in all things we are more than conquerors through him that loved us (Romans 8: 35-37).

Casting all your care upon him; for he careth for you (1 Peter 5:7).

And the peace of God, which passeth all understanding, shall keep your hearts and minds through Christ Jesus (Philippians 4:7).

When You Need...To Have A Better Self Image

Heavenly Father help me to have a healthy self-image of myself. Let me be confident in who I am and understand that God's love makes me valuable. Your word, Lord, says that I am precious in Your sight. Help me to understand who I am is determined by what God has declared about me and not by what others say about me. I pray that I am confident in my relationship with God and therefore I am secure in who I am, I do not give into thoughts and temptations of insecurity.

Lord, let me not filled with worry, anxiety or self doubts, but courage, boldness, and faith. I know I can do all things though Christ, who strengthens me. Help me think clearly and rationally and have a positive attitude. I will not allow the circumstances of life to steal my peace or joy. Show me how to see myself as You see me.

Your Word says I am more than a conqueror through Christ Jesus, that I am the head and not the tail, above and not beneath, going over and not under. Reveal to me how I can have strength to be victorious and triumphant in life. I am Your child and You have great plans for my life

Scriptures

Ye are of God, little children, and have overcome them: because greater is he that is in you, than he that is in the world (1 John 4:4).

Nay, in all things we are more than conquerors through him that loved us (Romans 8:37).

Being confident of this very thing, that he which hath begun a good work in you will perform it until the day of Jesus Christ (Philippians 1:6).

I can do all things through Christ which strengthen me (Philippians 4:13).

When You Need...Strength for Battle

Father God, in Jesus' name, I ask You to help me to not become weary in well doing. Help me to not be complacent or apathetic, but to be willing and obedient to do spiritual warfare when the need arises.

I proclaim that I am strong in You. I am empowered through my union with You. I draw strength from You for every battle that I face in life. I put on the whole armor today; therefore, I put myself in a position to successfully stand against all the strategies, deceits, and attacks of Satan and the forces of darkness. I recognize that I wrestle not against flesh and blood. No human being is my enemy. I will not direct my attack toward any person. My opponents are principalities, powers, and the rulers of the darkness of this world.

Because of Your armor, Lord, I am able to resist the enemy, stand my ground, and be victorious in the day of conflict and danger. When crisis comes to my life, I am bold to fight, to proclaim Your Word, and to stand upon Your promises. I firmly stand my ground and, having done all that the crisis may demand, I stand strong and hold my ground in the midst of the battle, knowing that ultimate victory is certain in You!

Scriptures

And let us not be weary in well doing: for in due season we shall reap, if we faint not (Galatians 6:9).

For we wrestle not against flesh and blood, but against principalities, against powers, against the rulers of the darkness of this world, against spiritual wickedness in high places (Ephesians 6:12).

Wherefore take unto you the whole armour of God, that ye may be able to withstand in the evil day, and having done all, to stand (Ephesians 6:13).

When You Need...Wisdom

Father, in Jesus' name, I come before You asking for Your wisdom. You said in Your Word that if anyone lacks wisdom, she could ask of You and You would give to her liberally. Lord, give me wisdom concerning my family, guidance and direction to properly manage my responsibilities, and discernment to balance worship, work, play, and rest in my life.

Lord, help me to operate in wisdom and understanding in every area of my life. No matter how small the task, Lord, I ask for Your wisdom to guide me. Before I undertake any new projects or consider any purchases, let Your wisdom teach me how to properly manage my time and to support my family.

When I am with my family or friends, let Your wisdom flow through me. Help me to speak Your words of encouragement and inspiration to them. Help me to take time to seek Your counsel and instruction before giving advice to anyone.

I thank You, Lord, that as I operate and function in wisdom my steps are ordered and directed of You. I am not easily swayed or convinced by emotionalism or by pressure from others; instead, I thank You for common sense, guidance, discernment, and truth functioning and flowing in my life. I thank You that by wisdom my house is established and that I have discretion in all my activities, in Jesus' name. Amen.

Scriptures

If any of you lack wisdom, let him ask of God, that giveth to all men liberally, and upbraideth not; and it shall be given him (James 1:5).

The steps of a good man are ordered by the Lord: and he delighteth in his way (Psalm 37:23).

Through wisdom is an house builded; and by understanding it is established (Proverbs 24:3).

IV

When You Are Facing...

When You Are Facing...A Crisis

Lord, help me to realize that crisis is normal in life. I desire to not become fearful, anxious, or overwhelmed when I find myself in a crisis situation. Help me to not react in confusion, worry, or desperation.

You said that in this world we would have tribulation but to be of good cheer because You have overcome the world. Help me to keep a good attitude and a cheerful heart no matter what I am facing.

You said that the afflictions of the righteous are many but that You deliver us out of them all. Deliver me out of this crisis; reveal to me Your plan of resolution. Help me to keep my mind fixed on You and the power of Your Word. Give me wisdom and insight concerning any decisions I need to make or actions I need to take to do my part in resolving this crisis.

I count it all joy when I am faced with trials and testing, knowing that the trying of my faith builds my patience and godly character. You have promised to deliver me, and I know You will. Give me courage, strength, and fortitude to not give up or give in but to patiently keep trusting You until my deliverance comes.

Thank You, Father, that I am free from this crisis in Jesus' name. Amen.

Scriptures

These things I have spoken unto you, that in me ye might have peace. In the world ye shall have tribulation: but be of good cheer; I have overcome the world (John 16:33).

Many are the afflictions of the righteous: but the Lord delivereth him out of them all (Psalm 34:19).

My brethren, count it all joy when ye fall into divers temptations; knowing this, that the trying of your faith worketh patience. But let patience have her perfect work, that ye may be perfect and entire, wanting nothing (James 1:2-4).

When You Are Facing...Discouragement

Lord, I pray in Jesus' name that You would help me to overcome this discouragement. Lord, I know that there is no problem too big, no hurt too deep, no mistake so bad that You cannot provide the power, strength, and wisdom to overcome it. You said in Your Word that many are the afflictions of the righteous but You will deliver them out of them all.

I ask for Your help, Lord. Give me courage and discernment to overcome the situation that I am facing. Restore my joy. Help me to trust You and to cast my cares, anxiety, and worries upon You. You tell me in Your Word that in this world I will have tribulation but to be of good cheer for You have overcome the world. You have made me a world overcomer. I refuse to let discouragement control my life.

Help me to replace my fears with faith, my doubts with belief, my worries with trust, and my cowardice with courage. Lord, help me to think the right things and to focus on You and not on my problems. Help me to rehearse Your goodness and to fill my heart with praise and thanksgiving for all that

You have done, are doing, and will do in my life. You have blessed me with so many wonderful blessings. Help me to be patient in times of difficulty. Give me endurance as I determine to not give up, cave in, or quit. I ask You, Lord, to give me Your joy as my strength. I have hope, confidence, and faith that You will see me through this situation and that what the enemy has meant for evil You shall turn for good.

Scriptures

> *Many are the afflictions of the righteous: but the Lord delivereth him out of them all (Psalm 34:19).*
>
> *These things I have spoken unto you, that in me ye might have peace. In the world ye shall have tribulation: but be of good cheer; I have overcome the world (John 16:33).*
>
> *Then he said unto them, Go your way, eat the fat, and drink the sweet, and send portions unto them for whom nothing is prepared: for this day is holy unto our Lord: neither be ye sorry; for the joy of the Lord is your strength (Nehemiah 8:10).*

But as for you, ye thought evil against me; but God meant it unto good, to bring to pass, as it is this day, to save much people alive (Genesis 50:20).

When You Are Facing...
Fatigue in my Body

Lord, I come to You in Jesus' name. I ask You for strength in my body. Restore to me energy and vitality to go on. Lord, I understand that mental frustrations and worries can bring on weariness and tiredness, so I cast every care in my life over on You. I ask You to strengthen my spirit, soul, and body today. I draw from Your encouragement and the power of Your Word. Just as David did, I encourage myself in You, O Lord. You are my strength, and You are my source of courage and resolve. Renew my strength, Lord.

Thank You for Your peace and rest. Help me to rest and do what is right for my body. I recognize that my body is the temple of Your Spirit. Help me to properly rest, exercise, and eat so I am not fighting against my body but helping to keep my body strong. I pray, Lord, that my youth would be renewed as the eagle's. Thank You for renewing Your strength within me.

Help me, Lord, to not become weak, weary, or faint in well doing but to gain strength through my union with You, that I might do, perform, and accomplish all that You have called me to do. Help me to not become tired, overworked, or stressed but to let Your joy fill my heart and strengthen my body. In Jesus' name I pray. Amen.

Scriptures

Cast thy burden upon the Lord, and he shall sustain thee: he shall never suffer the righteous to be moved (Psalm 55:22).

What? know ye not that your body is the temple of the Holy Ghost which is in you, which ye have of God, and ye are not your own? (1 Corinthians 6:19).

Who satisfieth thy mouth with good things; so that thy youth is renewed like the eagle's (Psalm 103:5).

And let us not be weary in well doing: for in due season we shall reap, if we faint not (Galatians 6:9).

When You Are Facing...Fear in Your Life

Dear Father, You have told me to not fear because You are with me, You uphold me, and You sustain me. I choose to trust in You instead of becoming fearful. Your Word says that though I walk through the valley of the shadow of death, I will fear no evil for Your rod and staff comfort me.

I will not be afraid of bad news, because You are my rock, my fortress, and my deliverer. You give me the strength and courage to handle any situation. You have promised that You would never leave me or forsake me.

I will not let the spirit of fear overtake me, for I choose not to give fear any place in my life. I stand strong in faith, and I choose to believe Your Word instead of the lies of the enemy.

In Your Word I find peace, wisdom, and instruction for any situation. Your Word says that You have given me power, love, and a sound mind. I will consider Your Word above the fear that tries to overtake me. When I am tempted to fear, I will look to You. In You, Lord, I am strong and fearless. In Jesus' name I pray. Amen.

Scriptures

Fear thou not; for I am with thee: be not dismayed; for I am thy God: I will strengthen thee; yea, I will help thee; yea, I will uphold thee with the right hand of my righteousness (Isaiah 41:10).

Yea, though I walk through the valley of the shadow of death, I will fear no evil: for thou art with me; thy rod and thy staff they comfort me (Psalm 23:4).

The Lord is my rock, and my fortress, and my deliverer; my God, my strength, in whom I will trust; my buckler, and the horn of my salvation, and my high tower (Psalm 18:2).

I will never leave thee, nor forsake thee (Hebrews 13:5).

For God hath not given us the spirit of fear; but of power, and of love, and of a sound mind (2 Timothy 1:7).

When You Are Facing...Procrastination

Lord, help me to overcome procrastination. Sometimes my duties and workload as a mother can overwhelm me, and I tend to procrastinate when I am faced with a major task before me. You said in Your Word to redeem the time. Whatever I do, I do it with all my might and am not tossed to and fro. Help me to be resolute in my decisions and strong in my convictions. Help me, Lord, to be disciplined to complete my tasks with excellence.

Lord, I choose to live my life with Your joy, and I choose to perform my duties with faithfulness. Whatever task is before me, I will do it to the best of my ability with a heart full of Your joy. Help me see the wisdom in performing the task at hand. Help me to not allow myself to become slothful or to become lazy in any way. Help me, Lord, to approach every task with a can-do attitude, and help me to develop the mental discipline to not put off till tomorrow what I can do today. I refuse to allow procrastination to control my life.

Thank You, Lord. I am free from procrastination today in Jesus' name! Amen.

Scriptures

Redeeming the time, because the days are evil (Ephesians 5:16).

Be...not slothful in business; fervent in spirit; serving the Lord (Romans 12:10-11).

Be not slothful, but followers of them who through faith and patience inherit the promises (Hebrews 6:12).

When You Are Facing... Rejection from Others

Lord, help me to not base my joy or happiness on what others think about me. Let me not be resentful or offended toward others, no matter what they may say or do to me.

Help me to not be discouraged or become emotionally distraught because of a suffered wrong. Heal my heart and emotions, Lord. Fill my soul with Your love, joy, and peace.

I refuse to be bitter or angry. I choose to walk in love and forgiveness. I will pray for those who have hurt and rejected me. Lord, speak to their hearts and minister to them. I will not retaliate or hold a grudge, but I cast the care of this situation over on You. I will not speak evil of them or gossip about them.

I thank You, Lord, that You will never leave me or forsake me. You are my best friend. You uphold me, You sustain me, and You have accepted me. Even though I may have been rejected by an individual, I know that I am accepted by You. Thank You for accepting me, in Jesus' name. Amen.

Scriptures

But I say unto you, Love your enemies, bless them that curse you, do good to them that hate you, and pray for them which despitefully use you, and persecute you (Matthew 5:44).

Casting all your care upon him; for he careth for you (1 Peter 5:7).

He hath said, I will never leave thee, nor forsake thee (Hebrews 13:5).

When You Are Facing... Spiritual Drought

Lord, sometimes it seems as if You are so far away. Lately I feel as if my prayers are without power and the cares of this world have choked my spiritual vitality.

O Lord, renew in me Your joy and strength. Give me back the joy of my salvation. By faith I receive Your love and mercy. No matter what I feel like, I know that You will never leave me or forsake me. By faith I encourage myself in You, Lord. I sing praises, hymns, and spiritual songs to You. I worship and adore You, Lord—not because of how I feel but because of who You are and my love for You. I am persuaded that neither death, nor life, nor angels, nor principalities, nor powers, nor things present, nor things to come, nor height, nor depth, nor any other creature shall be able to separate me from the love of God, which is in Christ Jesus my Lord.

I am alive unto You, Lord. Your joy is my strength. I trust You and boldly proclaim that Your goodness and mercy fill my life to overflowing. Let Your love, joy, and peace reign in my life. Strengthen me by the power of Your might. In Jesus' name I pray. Amen.

Scriptures

And the cares of this world, and the deceitfulness of riches, and the lusts of other things entering in, choke the word, and it becometh unfruitful (Mark 4:19).

Restore unto me the joy of thy salvation; and uphold me with thy free spirit (Psalm 51:12).

Let your conversation be without covetousness; and be content with such things as ye have: for he hath said, I will never leave thee, nor forsake thee (Hebrews 13:5).

Let the word of Christ dwell in you richly in all wisdom; teaching and admonishing one another in psalms and hymns and spiritual songs, singing with grace in your hearts to the Lord (Colossians 3:16).

For I am persuaded, that neither death, nor life, nor angels, nor principalities, nor powers, nor things present, nor things to come, nor height, nor depth, nor any other creature, shall be able to separate us from the love of God, which is in Christ Jesus our Lord (Romans 8:38-39).

When You Are Facing...Stress

Father, in the name of Jesus, I resist the stress that is in my life. I know that stress is harmful. I know that it is not Your will for me to be frustrated or fearful in anything. Lord, You said to cast all my cares over on You. Lord, I cast all my cares, all my anxieties, all my worry, and all my stress over on You. I receive Your peace in exchange.

Lord, help me to not worry. Help me, Lord, to not let circumstances or the frustration of daily living bring stress into my life or steal from me the joy You have placed within my heart. I know, Lord, that it is Your desire that I not be anxious, worried, or fretful over anything. I refuse to let stress dominate my life, and I thank You, Lord, that I am able to rise above the feeling of stress by the power of Your Holy Spirit in me.

You have promised in Your Word that You would give us peace that passes all understanding and that You would give us joy in the middle of problems, tests, and trials. I thank You for that joy and peace in my life. I refuse to live a life full of stress. Help me to focus on You and Your promises and not let stress affect or dominate my life.

Help me, Lord, to have patience in every situation, knowing that You are taking care of me, that You are working things out, and that I don't have to carry the anxiety, fear, or concern. I don't have to let stress be a destructive force in my life. I choose to walk peaceably, calmly, and confidently before You, knowing that You will provide all that I need. Through my union with You, I can live a stress-free life.

Scriptures

...casting all your care upon him; for he careth for you (1 Peter 5:7).

Do not be anxious about anything, but in everything, by prayer and petition, with thanksgiving, present your requests to God (Philippians 4:6 NIV).

And the peace of God, which transcends all understanding, will guard your hearts and your minds in Christ Jesus (Philippians 4:7 NIV).

When You Are Facing...Growing Older

Thank you Lord for the wonderful gift of life. Thank you for your faithfulness throughout my whole life. Thank you for helping me to navigate through the ups and downs, the good times and bad, the tragedies and triumphs of daily living. As I grow older show me how I can take the experiences of my life and use them to be a blessing to the next generation.

Reveal to me how to use the wisdom and insight I have gained to make a difference in the lives of those younger than me. Help me to forgive and forget those who have wronged me and to press on into the plan and purpose you have for me in the later years of my life. Help me to forget the past, enjoy the blessings of today, and look forward to what wonderful things you have in store for me in the next stage of my life. Keep me mentally alert, emotionally healthy, and spiritually strong. Show me where I can make the greatest contribution and have the most impact with my time. Help me be a mentor to young women, young wives, and young mothers. Give me wisdom how I can make a difference in their lives. Help to keep a positive outlook, a spring in my step, a song in my heart, and your joy in my spirit.

Scriptures

His lord said unto him, Well done, good and faithful servant; thou hast been faithful over a few things, I will make thee ruler over many things: enter thou into the joy of thy lord (Matthew 25:23).

For we wrestle not against flesh and blood, but against principalities, against powers, against the rulers of the darkness of this world, against spiritual wickedness in high places (Ephesians 6:12).

Wherefore take unto you the whole armour of God, that ye may be able to withstand in the evil day, and having done all, to stand (Ephesians 6:13).

For I am persuaded, that neither death, nor life, nor angels, nor principalities, nor powers, nor things present, nor things to come, nor height, nor depth, nor any other creature, shall be able to separate us from the love of God, which is in Christ Jesus our Lord (Romans 8:38-39).

When You Are Facing... Times of Adversity

Father, I thank You that even though at times I may be hedged in and pressed by oppressors on every side, even though I might be troubled and oppressed, I am never crushed.

Even though I may suffer embarrassments and be faced with perplexing situations, even though it seems as if I am unable to find my way out, I will never be driven to despair.

Even though I may be pursued, persecuted, and hard-driven, I know You will never leave me or forsake me. You will never desert me to stand alone.

Even though I may be struck down to the ground, I shall never be struck out or destroyed. You are with me, You are for me, and You are in me: This is the formula of success and victory for my life. I shall never give in, I shall never give up, and I shall never quit. My ultimate victory is guaranteed in You.

You said that in this world I would have tribulation but to be of good cheer because You have overcome this world.

You said that the afflictions of the righteous are many but You deliver them out of them all. Thank You, Lord, for delivering me from adversity.

Scriptures

We are troubled on every side, yet not distressed; we are perplexed, but not in despair; persecuted, but not forsaken; cast down, but not destroyed; always bearing about in the body the dying of the Lord Jesus, that the life also of Jesus might be made manifest in our body (2 Corinthians 4:8-10).

For he hath said, I will never leave thee, nor forsake thee (Hebrews 13:5).

These things I have spoken unto you, that in me ye might have peace. In the world ye shall have tribulation: but be of good cheer; I have overcome the world (John 16:33).

Many are the afflictions of the righteous: but the Lord delivereth him out of them all (Psalm 34:19).

When You Are Facing...Worry

Lord, You said in Your Word to not worry or have any anxiety about anything. You said to not take any thought or be concerned about any circumstance in my life. Lord, I cast my care, concern, and worry on You.

I refuse to worry or be fearful. I put my trust and confidence in You. I know You will take care of me. I know You love me. I thank You for Your presence. Grant to me Your peace that passes all understanding. You said not to let my heart be troubled or afraid. Help me, Lord, to keep my mind focused on You, knowing You will never leave me or forsake me.

Your Word says that the afflictions of the righteous are many but You deliver them out of them all. Let me keep looking to You and not worry or be in fear about the circumstances of my life. Lord, You said that in this world I would have tribulation, but You told me to be of good cheer because You have overcome the world and will help me to do the same.

Your Word says that all things work together for good to those who love You. I recognize that I can't do anything to change my circumstances by worrying, except to make them worse. I thank You, Lord, that what Satan has meant for evil You will turn for good. Thank You that I am free from worry, and I have victory in Jesus' name.

Scriptures

> *Be careful for nothing; but in every thing by prayer and supplication with thanksgiving let your requests be made known unto God (Philippians 4:6).*

> *Casting down imaginations, and every high thing that exalteth itself against the knowledge of God, and bringing into captivity every thought to the obedience of Christ (2 Corinthians 10:5).*

> *Casting all your care upon him; for he careth for you (1 Peter 5:7).*

> *And the peace of God, which passeth all understanding, shall keep your hearts and minds through Christ Jesus (Philippians 4:7).*

Many are the afflictions of the righteous: but the Lord delivereth him out of them all (Psalm 34:19).

These things I have spoken unto you, that in me ye might have peace. In the world ye shall have tribulation: but be of good cheer; I have overcome the world (John 16:33).

And we know that all things work together for good to them that love God, to them who are the called according to his purpose (Romans 8:28).

But as for you, ye thought evil against me; but God meant it unto good, to bring to pass, as it is this day, to save much people alive (Genesis 50:20).

V

My Home and Family

Godly Household

Lord, I thank You for Your presence in my home. I ask You to help me create an environment of peace, an environment that fosters a godly atmosphere. Let everyone who comes into my home sense the love, peace, and presence of God.

Help me to guard the atmosphere of my home by closely monitoring what kind of literature, music, movies, and television programs I allow in. I dedicate my home to You. Let every conversation and activity that takes place in this home honor You. I consecrate this home to Your glory for Your use. Let my home be a place of prayer, a place of safety, and a place of joy. Help me to use my home to minister Your life, Your love, and Your joy to all who enter here.

Give me discernment concerning the people I invite to visit or to live in my home. Help my home to always be a place of refuge and peace for all my family and friends. Let my home be a place that my children desire to come to and bring their friends to.

Thank You, Lord, for blessing me with my home. Help me to do my part in making it a special place for my family. May Your love reign supremely in this home, and may all who come through its doors find joy, comfort, and peace. In Jesus' name I pray. Amen.

Scriptures

As for me and my house, we will serve the Lord (Joshua 24:15).

And they shall teach my people the difference between the holy and profane, and cause them to discern between the unclean and the clean (Ezekiel 44:23).

And now abideth faith, hope, charity, these three; but the greatest of these is charity (1 Corinthians 13:13).

For My Husband

Lord, in Jesus' name, I thank You for the gift of my husband. I know You handpicked him just for me. I ask You to encourage him and strengthen his spirit, soul, and body. Give him wisdom and insight concerning every decision that he has to make, both personally and professionally.

Reveal Yourself to him. Speak to him by Your Spirit and through Your Word. Give him a hunger and thirst for righteousness. Shower him with Your love. Give him Your peace, joy, and strength regarding every aspect of his life.

Help him to be bold and confident in his faith. Send mentors and friends into his life who will offer godly encouragement and insight into his life and job.

Help me to be a spiritual, mental, and physical support to my husband. Let me be sensitive to his needs and be his best friend and greatest fan.

Scriptures

Blessed are they which do hunger and thirst after righteousness: for they shall be filled (Matthew 5:6).

Being confident of this very thing, that he which hath begun a good work in you will perform it until the day of Jesus Christ (Philippians 1:6).

Let us therefore follow after the things which make for peace, and things wherewith one may edify another (Romans 14:19).

Being a Godly Wife

Dear heavenly Father, develop in me Your character. I pray for Your wisdom and insight in all the matters of my life.

Help me to support and be a spiritual strength to my husband. Let me be sensitive to his needs. Show me ways that I can be an excellent help meet for him. Help me to encourage, inspire, and strengthen my husband. Help me to put a guard over my mouth so that I never criticize or condemn him. Help me to never say or do anything that would erode his confidence or self-image. Help me to reassure him in his faith and be supportive in his spiritual growth.

Lord, never let me be a nagging, overbearing, or demanding wife. Help me to walk in love and manifest the fruit of Your Spirit on a daily basis. Let me be quick to listen and slow to speak. Let my husband find a receptive and understanding heart in me.

Complete within me a godly nature. Help me to meditate on Your Word day and night. Let me create an atmosphere of Your presence in our home. Help me to be submissive and supportive in my role as a wife, recognizing that as I honor my husband, You, Lord, will bless my marriage. In Jesus' name I pray. Amen.

Scriptures

But the fruit of the Spirit is love, joy, peace, longsuffering, gentleness, goodness, faith, meekness, temperance: against such there is no law (Galatians 5:22-23).

But his delight is in the law of the Lord; and in his law doth he meditate day and night (Psalm 1:2).

Therefore as the church is subject unto Christ, so let the wives be to their own husbands in every thing (Ephesians 5:24).

Restoration for a Troubled Marriage

Lord, I know that You intended that the greatest, most rewarding human relationship in my life would be my marriage. Help my husband and me to resolve any differences that we have had. Rekindle in our hearts the love, joy, and passion we had for each other when we first were married. Lord, heal our hearts from the hurts of the past, and bring unity to our marriage.

Help us to forgive each other for mistakes we have made and to start fresh again. Help me to be loving, understanding, and sensitive toward my husband. Reveal to me areas where I need to change in order to improve our relationship.

Remind us and help us to never criticize or speak in anger to each other. Help us to put a guard over our mouths so that we never say words that bring hurt, pain, or discouragement to each other. Show us in Your Word, Lord, how to love and give to each other. Let our lives be an example of Your love and grace.

Lord, restore our marriage completely and totally in Jesus' name.

Scriptures

Brethren, I count not myself to have apprehended: but this one thing I do, forgetting those things which are behind, and reaching forth unto those things which are before (Philippians 3:13).

Let all bitterness, and wrath, and anger, and clamour, and evil speaking, be put away from you, with all malice (Ephesians 4:31).

My little children, let us not love in word, neither in tongue; but in deed and in truth (1 John 3:18).

Becoming A Godly Women

Lord, help me to glorify You in my role as a mother. Help me to be faithful to teach my children the truth and principles of Your Word. I desire to lead a godly life before them, being an example of the Christian walk. Help me to balance mercy and grace with correction and instruction.

Help me to be sensitive to my children's needs, to be understanding of their feelings, and to be fair and consistent in my discipline. I ask You for Your wisdom and discernment concerning all my decisions relating to my children. When I make a mistake, help me to be quick to ask for forgiveness.

Let me be an example of what to do when things go wrong, as well as when they go right. Help me to keep my cool and not become frustrated and lose my temper. If I do something that is wrong or offensive to my children, let me be quick to repent. Help me to instill within my children peace, consistency, and faithfulness. Help me to walk in love at all times and to be quick to provide encouragement, inspiration, and direction that will strengthen my children spiritually.

Give me patience and prudence to hear all sides of the story and not to jump to conclusions or react too quickly when faced with conflict among my children. Help me to recognize the gifts and talents that You have given them. Help me to cultivate and develop those gifts.

I pray that they will see You in me in every area of my life, Lord. In Jesus' name I pray. Amen.

Scriptures

We should live soberly, righteously, and godly, in this present world (Titus 2:12).

If any of you lack wisdom, let him ask of God, that giveth to all men liberally, and upbraideth not; and it shall be given him (James 1:5).

Be thou an example of the believers, in word, in conversation, in charity, in spirit, in faith, in purity (1 Timothy 4:12).

For My Baby

Dear Father, I pray in Jesus' name for my baby, __________. Thank You for this wonderful gift. One of the greatest joys in life is the privilege of being a mother. Help me, Lord, to be the kind of mother I need to be. Help me to be the godly influence that You desire in my baby's life. You have given me such a great and wonderful responsibility to mold, nurture, and mentor ____________. Let me show (him/her) Your love in every way.

When it comes time to correct ____________, help me to do so in love. Help me to provide an environment of peace and joy for __________. Lord, give me Your grace and mercy when I am tired, stressed, or feeling the pressures that the mother of a newborn often feels. Help me to not get discouraged. Help me to stay focused on the positive things in my life.

Help me to be all that ________ will need in a mother. Grant me the wisdom and discernment in every aspect of my relationship with __________. Help me to be sensitive to (his/her) needs. Help me to recognize the gifts and talents that You have placed within (him/her). Help me to do my part in helping ___________ to grow in them.

I speak blessings over _______________. I pray that You would bless (him/her) with grace, mercy, peace, favor, health, healing, strength, and vitality. I thank You, Lord, that ___________ will grow strong spiritually as (he/she) grows strong physically. I pray that no evil or harm shall come near ___________. I pray that (he/she) will follow You all the days of (his/her) life, and I pray that You would use ___________ to be a beacon of Your light, love, and hope to this world.

Scriptures

Lo, children are an heritage of the Lord: and the fruit of the womb is his reward (Psalm 127:3).

Provoke not your children to wrath: but bring them up in the nurture and admonition of the Lord (Ephesians 6:4).

There shall no evil befall thee, neither shall any plague come nigh thy dwelling. For he shall give his angels charge over thee, to keep thee in all thy ways. They shall bear thee up in their hands, lest thou dash thy foot against a stone (Psalm 91:10-12).

Being the Parent My Child Needs

Dear Lord, in Jesus' name I pray for my children. Thank You for giving them to me to teach and to love. Children are a blessing of the Lord.

I pray that I can be the mother my children need. Help me to guide and govern them. Help me to see them through Your eyes, to look past their imperfections and into their hearts.

Lord, let me not covet the things of this world for my children. Help me to teach them that character and honor matter more than being the best-dressed individual, the best athlete, or the most popular person.

Let me speak Your Word when my children need encouragement. Use me to show Your love and mercy to them.

I pray that my children will know You and serve You all the days of their lives.

Scriptures

Lo, children are an heritage of the Lord: and the fruit of the womb is his reward (Psalm 127:3).

But the Lord said unto Samuel, Look not on his countenance, or on the height of his stature; because I have refused him: for the Lord seeth not as man seeth; for man looketh on the outward appearance, but the Lord looketh on the heart (1 Samuel 16:7).

Wherefore comfort yourselves together, and edify one another, even as also ye do (1 Thessalonians 5:11).

Protection for My Children

Father God, I lift up my children before You. I ask You to watch over them. Hide them under the shadow of Your wings. Protect them from the evil in this world. Let no harm come to their spirits, souls, or bodies.

Lord, I thank You that Your angels go with and before my children. Thank You for protecting them and keeping them safe from danger, disease, and harm of every kind. Let no evil befall them. Let no plague come near them. I thank You, Lord, that my children are safe in the shelter of Your arms.

Protect my children from injury of any kind. I pray that they would be sensitive to Your Spirit and that You would direct their steps. Give my children courage to say no to friends and activities that would put them in danger.

I thank You, Lord, that You protect them from spiritual, mental, physical, and emotional abuse from others. You protect them from the enemy's evil plans to bring them harm because Your Word says that the evil one touches them not and that no weapon formed against them shall prosper.

I thank You, Lord, that water shall not overtake them and fire shall not consume them. Wherever they go and whatever they do, You protect them, Lord. In Jesus' name I proclaim it. Amen.

Scriptures

> *Because thou hast been my help, therefore in the shadow of thy wings will I rejoice (Psalm 63:7).*

> *There shall no evil befall thee, neither shall any plague come nigh thy dwelling. For he shall give his angels charge over thee, to keep thee in all thy ways (Psalm 91:10-11).*

> *No weapon that is formed against thee shall prosper; and every tongue that shall rise against thee in judgment thou shalt condemn. This is the heritage of the servants of the Lord, and their righteousness is of me, saith the Lord (Isaiah 54:17).*

Correcting My Children

Lord, I understand that correction is a vital part of my relationship with my children. I pray for Your wisdom and counsel regarding the proper ways and times to correct my children. Help me to never correct out of anger or frustration but to calmly and objectively address the situation.

Help me to teach my children that Your Word is the standard by which they are to conduct their lives. Help me to always correct in love. Before, during, and after any time of correction, help me to always reinforce my love for them. In those times, help them to understand that, even though I am displeased with their behavior, I love them totally, completely, and unconditionally. Help me to always ensure that the punishment fits the crime and not make emotional or irrational decisions.

Help me to be kind and understanding, knowing that my children are in the process of changing and growing. Also, give me courage to address problems when necessary and not be passive or too lenient in areas just because I do not want to deal with them. Help me to understand that Your Word says that if I refuse to correct my children, then I do not love them. Help me, Lord, to set standards for their behavior and lifestyle that are in line with Your Word.

Help me to balance correction and discipline with Your mercy and grace. In Jesus' name I pray. Amen.

Scriptures

And he said unto them, Set your hearts unto all the words which I testify among you this day, which ye shall command your children to observe to do, all the words of this law (Deuteronomy 32:46).

If thy children will keep my covenant and my testimony that I shall teach them, their children shall also sit upon thy throne for evermore (Psalm 132:12).

For whom the Lord loveth he correcteth; even as a father the son in whom he delighteth (Proverbs 3:12).

My Child's School & Teachers

Lord, I pray for my children's school. I pray for the principal, the administrative staff, and all of the teachers. I ask You to encourage and strengthen their spirits, souls, and bodies. Draw them close to You.

For those who do not know You, I pray that the eyes of their understanding would be opened, that their hearts would be receptive to the Gospel, and that they would come to a saving knowledge of You. For those who are in relationship with You, I pray that You would give them boldness to be witnesses for You. Let Your Word come alive in their hearts. Let them be contagious with Your love, life, and hope.

I ask You to give the teachers at the school wisdom, insight, and direction to effectively and efficiently perform their duties. Give them understanding, patience, and discernment to relate to their students and to be a positive influence in their lives. Help them to see the potential in each student, and give them the ability to bring out the best in them. Help them to recognize and encourage the gifts and talents that

You have placed within each student. Help them to balance instruction, correction, and mercy. Help them to create a fun, exciting, and stimulating atmosphere for learning.

Lord, help me to partner with the school and with the teachers to provide the best possible learning experience for my children. In Jesus' name I pray. Amen.

Scriptures

The eyes of your understanding being enlightened; that ye may know what is the hope of his calling, and what the riches of the glory of his inheritance in the saints (Ephesians 1:18).

Having then gifts differing according to the grace that is given to us... (Romans 12:6).

I will instruct thee and teach thee in the way which thou shalt go: I will guide thee with mine eye (Psalm 32:8).

Future of My Children

Lord, I pray for my children in Jesus' name. I pray that You would reveal to them the desires and plans that You have for them. Fulfill Your plans and purposes in their lives. Kindle a passion in their hearts to pursue the course that You have prepared for them. Send the right friends and teachers and influences into their lives to encourage, inspire, and motivate them to seek Your will for their lives, to be strong in their convictions, and to be bold witnesses for You.

Bring to completion the work that You have begun in them. Use them to do many great things for Your kingdom. Use them to be a positive influence in the lives of their friends and acquaintances.

Holy Spirit, lead, guide, and direct their steps. Speak to their hearts, and make it clear to their minds the destiny that God has prepared for them. Help me to play the part that You have for me to play as their mother—to encourage them and foster within them the desire to pursue the assignment that You have called them to. Lord, give them courage and strength to overcome any obstacles in their quest to fulfill Your will.

Give them patience and persistence, and help them balance both so that they can wait when necessary, yet courageously pursue as You direct. Help them to not lose heart or give up when they face setbacks but with strong resolution to be bold and be strong in their faith. Give them fortitude to press on when they are tempted to give up and quit.

Lord, use them to make a difference in the lives of all the people they know. May their lives be a testimony of Your love, Your passion, and Your abundant provision. In Jesus' name I pray. Amen.

Scriptures

Being confident of this very thing, that he which hath begun a good work in you will perform it until the day of Jesus Christ (Philippians 1:6).

For the gifts and calling of God are without repentance (Romans 11:29).

Therefore, since we have such a hope, we are very bold (2 Corinthians 3:12 NIV).

My Child's Hunger for God

Father, I pray that You would give my children a hunger for You. Let them desire to serve You and to know You. I pray that they will come to know You on a personal level as they see Your goodness and mercy.

Send my children godly friends and people who will lead them to You, Lord, and not away from You. Teach them by the Holy Spirit to hear and know Your voice, Lord.

I pray that my children will hunger and thirst for righteousness. The Bible says that we can know the depths and heights of Your love. I pray that my children will set a time to read and study Your Word so that they can come to know You in Your wholeness. Let them be disciplined to spend time with You.

I pray that my children will look to You to direct their paths. When a situation arises, let them think immediately about how the Bible addresses it.

Give them the courage to speak Your Word in boldness and confidence. Help them to overcome obstacles by taking the Bible and applying it to their lives. In Jesus' name I pray. Amen.

Scriptures

Blessed are they which do hunger and thirst after righteousness: for they shall be filled (Matthew 5:6).

That Christ may dwell in your hearts by faith; that ye, being rooted and grounded in love, may be able to comprehend with all saints what is the breadth, and length, and depth, and height (Ephesians 3:17-18).

In all thy ways acknowledge him, and he shall direct thy paths (Proverbs 3:6).

My Child's Spiritual Growth

Lord, I pray for my children. I ask You to draw them closer to You. I pray that they would be sensitive to Your Spirit. Put a desire in their hearts to know You. Make Your Word come alive to them. Reveal the wonders of Your character to them. Lead, guide, and direct them into Your perfect will for their lives.

I pray that my children would grow strong in faith. Give them courage to be witnesses for You. Let Your light, love, and life shine through them. Encourage them and strengthen them spiritually. Give them boldness and courage to follow You without compromise.

Holy Spirit, bring to my children's remembrance the Word of God. When they are pressured to make decisions that are not Your will for their lives, give them the strength to make the right choices.

I pray that my children would fulfill the plans and purposes that You have for them. Thank You, Lord, that their minds are fixed on You and they will follow You all the days of their lives. In Jesus' name I pray. Amen.

Scriptures

He restoreth my soul: he leadeth me in the paths of righteousness for his name's sake (Psalm 23:3).

But the Comforter, which is the Holy Ghost, whom the Father will send in my name, he shall teach you all things, and bring all things to your remembrance, whatsoever I have said unto you (John 14:26).

For I know the thoughts that I think toward you, saith the Lord, thoughts of peace, and not of evil, to give you an expected end (Jeremiah 29:11).

Nighttime Prayer for My Children

Father, in Jesus' name, I pray for my children. I thank You for the wonderful gift they are to my life and this family. I pray that You give them a restful and refreshing night's sleep, free from worries, anxiety, and nightmares. I ask You to encourage and strengthen my children's spirits, souls, and bodies.

Reveal Yourself to my children by Your Spirit and through Your Word. Draw them close to You. May they come to know You more intimately. Help them to be sensitive to Your voice. I pray that they will honor You by the decisions that they make and the words that they speak.

Give them courage to stand up for what is right and to stand against what is wrong. Help them to be strong in spirit so that they are able to resist temptation and peer pressure. Lord, develop within them hearts of purity. Help them to follow their convictions.

Protect my children, and keep them safe from harm and evil of every kind. I pray for Your healing power in my children's lives. Keep them healed, whole, and healthy.

Reveal to my children the plans and purposes that You have for their lives. Grant them the courage to pursue Your will.

Scriptures

I will both lay me down in peace, and sleep: for thou, Lord, only makest me dwell in safety (Psalm 4:8).

Fear thou not; for I am with thee: be not dismayed; for I am thy God: I will strengthen thee; yea, I will help thee; yea, I will uphold thee with the right hand of my righteousness (Isaiah 41:10).

For I know the thoughts that I think toward you, saith the Lord, thoughts of peace, and not of evil, to give you an expected end (Jeremiah 29:11).

For My Teenager

Lord, I pray for _____________. Reveal Yourself to __________. Draw (him/her) close to You, and put a hunger in (his/her) heart for You.

I ask You to encourage and strengthen __________'s spirit, soul, and body. Help (him/her) to be strong and resolute in (his/her) convictions when (he/she) is faced with temptation. Instill within __________ a boldness and confidence in You and Your Word. Give __________ discernment and wisdom concerning the choices that (he/she) makes.

Help ___________ to have courage to live a godly life and to walk in Your paths. Let __________ boldly say no to drugs, premarital sex, and any temptation that would try to lure (him/her) away from a godly lifestyle. Help _________ to have a healthy self-image and to be strong when faced with peer pressure.

Reveal to __________ the plans and purposes that You have for (his/her) life, and give _____________ the courage and boldness to pursue (his/her) God-given destiny. Give

__________ wisdom and insight to develop the gifts and talents You have placed within (him/her).

Lord, I pray against bad influences in __________'s life. Remove from ______________ those who are harming or negatively influencing (him/her). Help ____________ to see sin for what it is, and help (him/her) to stand against evil influences.

I pray that Your angels would take charge over ____________. I pray for protection over ____________ everywhere that (he/she) may go.

Thank You, Lord, that ___________ is fulfilling Your call, in Jesus' name. Amen.

Scriptures

For I know the thoughts that I think toward you, saith the Lord, thoughts of peace, and not of evil, to give you an expected end (Jeremiah 29:11).

Praying always with all prayer and supplication in the Spirit, and watching thereunto with all perseverance and supplication for all saints; and for me, that utterance may be given unto me, that I may open my mouth boldly, to make known the mystery of the gospel (Ephesians 6:18-19).

For he shall give his angels charge over thee, to keep thee in all thy ways (Psalm 91:11).

Teenager to Return to God

Father, in Jesus' name, I lift up ________ to You. I pray that You would open the eyes of (his/her) understanding. Show _________ what is good and acceptable before You, and encourage and strengthen (him/her) to pursue You. Lord, I pray that the voice of Your Spirit would become stronger and louder than the voice of the world in _________'s heart and mind. I rebuke the devil and the forces of darkness that would try to steal (his/her) life and (his/her) relationship with You.

I train up _____________ in the way (he/she) should go, and I thank You that when (he/she) is old (he/she) will not depart from it. Lord, remove from ____________ those who are harming or negatively influencing (him/her). Help ___________ to see sin for what it is, and help (him/her) to stand against peer pressure and evil influences. I pray that You would speak to _______________'s heart. Encourage (him/her) to do right. Give _________ strength and wisdom to say no to the wrong choices. Surround (him/her) with godly friends who will be a strong spiritual influence in (his/her) life. Bring ____________ strong adult influences, such as teachers, coaches, and others who will encourage (him/her) to follow You and to conduct (his/her) life in a way that honors You. Restore to ______________ a tender heart that loves You and desires to follow You.

Give me discernment and wisdom to know what role I am to play to influence ______________ to live a godly life. Help me to be resolute in my standards but never condescending, critical, or condemning of ________________. Help me to properly communicate my unconditional love, my concern, and the value and benefit of living a godly life before You.

Thank You, Father, in Jesus' name, ______________ will love and serve You all the days of (his/her) life. Amen.

Scriptures

The eyes of your understanding being enlightened; that ye may know what is the hope of his calling, and what the riches of the glory of his inheritance in the saints (Ephesians 1:18).

Train up a child in the way he should go: and when he is old, he will not depart from it (Proverbs 22:6).

Let no corrupt communication proceed out of your mouth, but that which is good to the use of edifying, that it may minister grace unto the hearers (Ephesians 4:29).

Observing Family Communion

Father, we come to You in Jesus' name. We thank You for Jesus, the sacrificial Lamb, the atonement and redemption for the sins of all humanity.

In obedience to You, we observe the practice of Holy Communion. We examine our lives and ask You to forgive us for any sin or iniquity in our hearts. We thank You for the juice, which represents the blood You shed for the remission of sins. Lord, we know the blood represents a new covenant, a better covenant, a covenant of redemption and grace. Thank You for redeeming us and receiving us as Your own children.

We thank You for the bread, which represents Your body that was broken, bruised, and led to death as a sacrifice for us. You took stripes on Your body so we could receive healing. As we eat this bread, we thank You, Lord, for health and healing in our bodies. We thank You for strength and vitality. We thank You for restoration of wholeness—spirit, soul, and body.

We thank You, Lord, that Your resurrection power is working in our lives today. In Jesus' name we pray. Amen.

Scriptures

Jesus took bread, and blessed it, and brake it, and gave it to the disciples, and said, Take, eat; this is my body. And he took the cup, and gave thanks, and gave it to them, saying, Drink ye all of it; for this is my blood of the new testament, which is shed for many for the remission of sins (Matthew 26:26-28).

Because of this oath, Jesus has become the guarantee of a better covenant (Hebrews 7:22 NIV).

But he was wounded for our transgressions, he was bruised for our iniquities: the chastisement of our peace was upon him; and with his stripes we are healed (Isaiah 53:5).

Losing a Loved One

Dear heavenly Father, I come before You with sadness in my heart. I have lost a loved one and need Your strength.

Help me, Lord, to overcome this grief and despair. I cannot do it on my own. I call on Your Holy Spirit, who lives inside of me, to comfort me. Your Word says that nothing can separate us from the love of Christ—not trouble or hardship or persecution or famine or nakedness or danger or sword, not death or life, angels or demons, the present or the future.

I understand that grief is a process. Help me to walk through this process without giving in to despair. Give me the strength to praise You even though I may not feel like it.

You are my hiding place and my strong tower. You are an ever-present help in times of trouble. Your joy is my strength. Your comfort sustains me. Your peace keeps my soul from anguish. You are my hope and my victory. In Jesus' name I pray. Amen.

Scriptures

But the Comforter, which is the Holy Ghost, whom the Father will send in my name, he shall teach you all things, and bring all things to your remembrance, whatsoever I have said unto you (John 14:26).

Who shall separate us from the love of Christ? Shall trouble or hardship or persecution or famine or nakedness or danger or sword? For I am convinced that neither death nor life, neither angels nor demons, neither the present nor the future, nor any powers, neither height nor depth, nor anything else in all creation, will be able to separate us from the love of God that is in Christ Jesus our Lord (Romans 8:35,38,39 NIV).

VI

My Relationships

Walking in Love

Lord, You have commanded us to walk in love. Help me to fulfill that commandment.

Father, in Jesus' name, I commit to walk in love. I pray that I will not take offense when someone does me wrong. Help me to see others through Your eyes of love. Let me be compassionate to those who do not know You and Your love.

Let me minister Your love everywhere I go. As I walk in love, people are blessed and lives are changed. Let people see You through me.

Your Word says that because I love, I endure long, I am patient, and I am kind. I am never envious and never boil over with jealousy. I am not boastful or vainglorious, and I do not display myself haughtily. I am not rude and unmannerly, and I do not act unbecomingly. I do not insist on my own rights or my own way, for I am not self-seeking, touchy, fretful, or resentful. I take no account of an evil done to me; I pay no attention to a suffered wrong. I do not rejoice at injustice and unrighteousness, but I rejoice when right and truth prevail. I bear up under anything and everything that comes. I am ever ready to believe the best of others. My hopes are fadeless under all circumstances. I endure everything without weakening because my love never fails.

You are love, and You are in me, so I pray that Your love will be manifested in my life. I pray that I will become a channel of Your love to my world. In Jesus' name I pray. Amen.

Scriptures

This is my commandment, That ye love one another, as I have loved you (John 15:12).

Charity suffereth long, and is kind; charity envieth not; charity vaunteth not itself, is not puffed up, doth not behave itself unseemly, seeketh not her own, is not easily provoked, thinketh no evil; rejoiceth not in iniquity, but rejoiceth in the truth; beareth all things, believeth all things, hopeth all things, endureth all things. Charity never faileth (1 Corinthians 13:4-8).

No man hath seen God at any time. If we love one another, God dwelleth in us, and his love is perfected in us (1 John 4:12).

Communication With Others

Lord, I recognize that my ability to communicate with others is a vital ingredient to developing and maintaining my relationship with them. Help me to be an effective communicator. Teach me to be a good listener and to be sensitive to the needs of my family and friends. Help me to effectively communicate my heart.

Help me to be quick to listen and slow to speak. Let me never speak out of anger or frustration. When I speak to my children, help me to not be judgmental or condemning. When anyone comes to me with a problem or concern, help me to not be so eager to give advice or solutions that I really don't take time to hear what is being said to me.

Help me to properly discern how I am to respond. Give me the proper words to say that accurately convey the feelings of my heart without ever being offensive or rude to others. In Jesus' name I pray. Amen.

Scriptures

Wherefore, my beloved brethren, let every man be swift to hear, slow to speak, slow to wrath (James 1:19).

I said, I will take heed to my ways, that I sin not with my tongue: I will keep my mouth with a bridle. (Psalm 39:1).

Who is a wise man and endued with knowledge among you? let him shew out of a good conversation his works with meekness of wisdom (James 3:13).

Forgiveness

Father, in Jesus' name, I pray for those individuals who have hurt me in the past. As an act of my will, I forgive them for what they did. I will not hate them, despise them, or desire that they suffer retribution for their actions. In fact, Lord, I ask You to forgive them and open their eyes so that they will see and know the error of their ways and not hurt others in the way that they hurt me. Draw them close to You, Lord. Minister Your life unto them.

I give You all the hurt and bitterness in my life. I refuse to carry the burden of those past hurts in my heart anymore. Help me, Lord, to cleanse my heart with Your Word. I release the individuals who have hurt me, and I ask You to speak Your blessings upon them. I will no longer live with the suffered wrong. I resist the temptation to pick up or remember the hurts. I will not gossip about what they did or ridicule or attack their character. Instead, I choose to think on Your Word, which tells me to let go of the past and press on toward the prize of Your high calling.

I will not let the pain of my past rob me of the promise of my future.

Thank You, Lord, for freeing me from my past. In Jesus' name I pray. Amen.

Scriptures

And forgive us our debts, as we forgive our debtors (Matthew 6:12).

Remember ye not the former things, neither consider the things of old (Isaiah 43:18).

Brethren, I count not myself to have apprehended: but this one thing I do, forgetting those things which are behind, and reaching forth unto those things which are before, I press toward the mark for the prize of the high calling of God in Christ Jesus (Philippians 3:13-14).

Favor

Dear heavenly Father, You said in Your Word that if my ways please You, then even my enemies will be at peace with me. Help me to live my life in such a manner that is pleasing to You. You said in Your Word that if I would honor You, then You would honor me and bring favor on my life.

Lord, I honor You and exalt You and give You first place in my life. I thank You that Your favor opens doors that men cannot shut. I know that Your favor creates opportunities and brings blessing to every area of my life. Lord, I thank You that Your favor is a crown on my head and a shield that goes before me.

Your favor, goodness, and mercy cover and surround me like a cloud and bring peace, fulfillment, and joy to my life. Thank You, Lord, for favor in Jesus' name.

Scriptures

When a man's ways please the Lord, he maketh even his enemies to be at peace with him (Proverbs 16:7).

For surely, O Lord, you bless the righteous; you surround them with your favor as with a shield (Psalm 5:12 NIV*).*

I know thy works: behold, I have set before thee an open door, and no man can shut it. (Revelation 3:8).

Choosing the Right Friends

Father, help me to develop godly relationships in my life. Give me discernment concerning the friendships I make.

Lord, I realize the wrong friendships can be a destructive force in my life. Help me to let go of any relationship that pulls me away from You and Your Word. Help me to recognize any relationship in my life that is codependent, and give me insight to correct or end that relationship.

Lead me to friends who love You and have a close relationship with You. Help me to be sensitive to the needs of my friends and to encourage them in their spiritual walk. May You, Lord, be at the center of all my friendships.

Lord, help me to develop honest, trustworthy, and loyal friendships. Help us to speak the truth about areas in each other's life that need improvement. Help us to not be offended but thankful that we love each other enough to speak the truth.

Give me Your wisdom, Lord, to build relationships that will last a lifetime. In Jesus' name I pray. Amen.

Scriptures

If any of you lacks wisdom, he should ask God, who gives generously to all without finding fault, and it will be given to him (James 1:5 NIV)

He who walks with the wise grows wise, but a companion of fools suffers harm (Proverbs 13:20 NIV).

But speaking the truth in love, may grow up into him in all things, which is the head, even Christ: From whom the whole body fitly joined together and compacted by that which every joint supplieth, according to the effectual working in the measure of every part, maketh increase of the body unto the edifying of itself in love (Ephesians 4:15-16).

For Another's Salvation

Father, in the name of Jesus, I pray for ________ to come to know Jesus as Lord and Savior. I know that You desire for all those who are lost to come to You.

Send Christians across __________'s path to minister Your love and grace to (him/her). Let ___________ hear the message of the Gospel clearly and accurately. Lord, prepare ________'s heart so that (he/she) is receptive to Your Word. Open __________'s spiritual eyes that (he/she) might see, know, and understand how much You love (him/her).

Make it clear to me the role I am to play. Give me opportunities to share my faith. Help me to do so at the right time, in the right place, and with sensitivity so that I am able to encourage ________ to accept You and receive salvation.

I rebuke the devil and his every attempt to stop, influence, or hinder _________ from making a decision to accept You, Lord, as (his/her) personal Savior.

Father, I thank You that ________ is a child of God, in Jesus' name.

Scriptures

For God so loved the world, that he gave his only begotten Son, that whosoever believeth in him should not perish, but have everlasting life (John 3:16).

Pray ye therefore the Lord of the harvest, that he will send forth labourers into his harvest (Matthew 9:38).

The eyes of your understanding being enlightened; that ye may know what is the hope of his calling, and what the riches of the glory of his inheritance in the saints (Ephesians 1:18).

Submit yourselves therefore to God. Resist the devil, and he will flee from you (James 4:7).

Relationships

Father, show me how to have healthy relationships with my friends and family. Help me to choose Godly friends who will uplift my spirit and encourage me. Show me how to discern harmful relationships of potential friends and give me friends who will have my best interests at heart.

Help me to see my family and friends through Your eyes and not with all the baggage of my past with them. Let me be a positive influence in their lives using kind and compassionate words, when they need a listening hear. Reveal to me how to guard against using the words I speak to tare down someone instead of build them up. Lord, I pray that my friendships will glorify You in every way.

Scriptures

A man that hath friends must show himself friendly: and there is a friend that sticketh closer than a brother (Proverbs 18:24).

Let the word of Christ dwell in you richly in all wisdom; teaching and admonishing one another in psalms an hyms and spiritual songs, singing and grace in your hearts to the Lord. (Colossians 3:16)

Ye are my friends if ye do whatsoever I command you. (John 15:14)

Be thou an example of the believers, in word, in conversation, in charity, in spirit, in faith, in purity (1 Timothy 4:12).

VII

Living My Life Everyday

Divine Protection

Dear heavenly Father, I pray for protection for my family and for myself. I know that You said in Your Word that You would never leave us or forsake us. I believe that Your angels go before us to protect us and keep us from harm and danger of any kind.

Lord, Your Word says that You hide us under Your wings, that no evil shall befall me or my family, and that no plague or calamity shall come near my home.

I pray for safety over our home and our vehicles. Wherever we go and whatever we do, I thank You that we operate in Your divine protection. I pray for safety on the highways as we travel to school, to work, to church, and to our every destination. I pray that You protect our home from burglaries and vandalism. I pray that You protect my children from any threats of physical, mental, or emotional violence.

Father, I pray for Your peace that passes all understanding to guard over our hearts and minds. Thank You for Your protection in every area of our lives, in Jesus' name. Amen.

Scriptures

Let your conversation be without covetousness; and be content with such things as ye have: for he hath said, I will never leave thee, nor forsake thee (Hebrews 13:5).

Keep me as the apple of the eye, hide me under the shadow of thy wings (Psalm 17:8).

There shall no evil befall thee, neither shall any plague come nigh thy dwelling (Psalm 91:10).

And the peace of God, which passeth all understanding, shall keep your hearts and minds through Christ Jesus (Philippians 4:7).

Safety for Travel

Dear heavenly Father, I pray for Your protection as I travel today. Your Word says that You give Your angels charge over me, and I commission Your angels to go with me and before me, to protect me and keep me from harm and injury and evil of any kind.

Lord, Your Word says that no weapon formed against me shall prosper, that no evil thing shall befall me, and that no plague shall come near me. Thank You, Lord, that I travel in Your divine protection. According to Your Word, even in the midst of calamity and destruction, You will preserve me and keep me safe.

I thank You that if at any time my life is in danger of any kind, I am sensitive to the voice of the Holy Spirit and You direct me out of the path of harm and keep me in Your hand of safety. I trust You to speak clearly to my heart if You need me to make any changes in my travel plans. Otherwise, I go in peace, knowing that Your preserving power accompanies me everywhere I go.

I thank You that my vehicle operates and functions properly and that the person in the driver's seat is alert and attentive. I thank You that everyone involved in my travel operates in wisdom and understanding at all times.

Lord, I thank You that I travel in safety in Jesus' name. Amen.

Scriptures

For he shall give his angels charge over thee, to keep thee in all thy ways (Psalm 91:11).

No weapon that is formed against thee shall prosper; and every tongue that shall rise against thee in judgment thou shalt condemn. This is the heritage of the servants of the Lord, and their righteousness is of me, saith the Lord (Isaiah 54:17).

Thou art my hiding place; thou shalt preserve me from trouble; thou shalt compass me about with songs of deliverance. Selah (Psalm 32:7).

Staying Physically Fit

Lord, I understand that my body is the temple of the Holy Spirit. I understand that I am to be a good steward over my body and make sure I stay physically fit.

You told me in Your Word to present my body a living sacrifice, holy and pleasing to You. I recognize that if I am overweight and out of shape it will affect my ability to serve my family, my friends, and the work of the Gospel.

Your Word also says that if I walk in the Spirit, I will not fulfill the lust of my flesh. Holy Spirit, guide me in choosing the eating and exercise program that is best for me. Help me to make conscious lifestyle choices that will cause my body to function in health and vitality. Give me determination and courage to say no to health-destroying foods and substances. Show me how to incorporate a daily exercise routine into my schedule, and help me to discipline my body to follow that plan.

I thank You, Lord, for a healthy and fit body. I rejoice in the results I will see as I exercise and subject myself to You. In Jesus' name I pray. Amen.

Scriptures

What? know ye not that your body is the temple of the Holy Ghost which is in you, which ye have of God, and ye are not your own? (1 Corinthians 6:19).

I beseech you therefore, brethren, by the mercies of God, that ye present your bodies a living sacrifice, holy, acceptable unto God, which is your reasonable service (Romans 12:1).

This I say then, Walk in the Spirit, and ye shall not fulfil the lust of the flesh (Galatians 5:16).

Healthy Eating Habits

Dear Father, I understand that the food we eat plays one of the most important roles in our health and the proper functioning of our bodies.

Help me to be sensible and use wisdom regarding what type of food I eat. Help me to not eat out of habit or for social enjoyment, but only when I am hungry.

Help me to glorify You in my body and not eat foods that bring sickness, disease, or harm to my body. Help me to be disciplined to not overeat or eat late at night. Lord, I ask You to help me control my appetite instead of indulging my flesh. Lord, give me wisdom to choose the best eating plan for me and my family.

Help me to not let the lust of my flesh control and dictate my eating habits. Before I eat anything, help me to consider the nutritional value and benefit, or the harm that the food will bring to my body. Help me to develop healthy eating habits so my body will be strong and healthy, that I may fulfill the plans and purposes You have for me. In Jesus' name I pray. Amen.

Scriptures

If any of you lack wisdom, let him ask of God, that giveth to all men liberally, and upbraideth not; and it shall be given him (James 1:5).

For, brethren, ye have been called unto liberty; only use not liberty for an occasion to the flesh, but by love serve one another (Galatians 5:13).

For ye are bought with a price: therefore glorify God in your body, and in your spirit, which are God's (1 Corinthians 6:20).

Time Management

Lord, the responsibilities and demands of my life seem overwhelming at times. Many days I feel as if my life is running me instead of me running it. Please help me in the selection and management of the right priorities for my life. Help me to not procrastinate but to be diligent to fulfill my responsibilities in a timely manner.

Lord, help me to set boundaries and not overcommit. Above all, help me to make sure I make time for You first. Help me to set my schedule so that prayer, worship, and Scripture study are a prominent part of my day.

Help me redeem the time to find ways to be more effective and efficient in my daily activities. Give me strength to say no to requests and activities that threaten to steal time from my higher priorities. If I start to slip out of my schedule or begin to neglect my priorities, then speak to my heart and prompt me to stay on track. In Jesus' name I pray. Amen.

Scriptures

But his delight is in the law of the Lord; and in his law doth he meditate day and night (Psalm 1:2).

He becometh poor that dealeth with a slack hand: but the hand of the diligent maketh rich (Proverbs 10:4).

Walk in wisdom toward them that are without, redeeming the time (Colossians 4:5).

Finances

Dear Father, I know that it is Your will to bless me. I know that as I am faithful to pay my tithes and give to Your work, You will bless me. You said that as I give it shall be given back to me, good measure, pressed down, and shaken together.

Your Word says that You love a cheerful giver. Help me to be sensitive to Your Spirit, and help me to be obedient to give as You instruct me. Give me wisdom and understanding, that I might be a good steward over all that You have given me. Help me to use discretion in my spending habits. Let me be practical, sensible, and intelligent in all my buying decisions.

Give me creative ideas and new insight to create income for my family. Help me to be productive and diligent in my job. Give me favor with my employer.

I thank You, Lord, that increase and promotion come from You. I thank You that I and my family are blessed. Let us be financially successful so that we can be abundant givers to Your work and a blessing to others. In Jesus' name I pray. Amen.

Scriptures

Bring ye all the tithes into the storehouse, that there may be meat in mine house, and prove me now herewith, saith the Lord of hosts, if I will not open you the windows of heaven, and pour you out a blessing, that there shall not be room enough to receive it (Malachi 3:10).

Every man according as he purposeth in his heart, so let him give; not grudgingly, or of necessity: for God loveth a cheerful giver (2 Corinthians 9:7).

He that diligently seeketh good procureth favour: but he that seeketh mischief, it shall come unto him (Proverbs 11:27).

For promotion cometh neither from the east, nor from the west, nor from the south. But God is the judge: he putteth down one, and setteth up another (Psalm 75:6-7).

Giving

Lord, I thank You for blessing me with the joyful opportunity to give to Your kingdom. Everything I have comes from You. It is a privilege to give money and resources to Your work so that others might hear the good news of the Gospel.

Lord, I don't give to get; I give to honor You and to be a blessing to others. Your Word says that if I am faithful to give of my substance, then You will bless me and my family. Thank You for providing for my every need. I thank You that as I tithe, You open the windows of heaven and pour out abundant and overwhelming blessings on me.

You promised to rebuke the devourer for my sake. You promised that whatever I do for others You would make happen for me. You said that the righteous would never have to beg for what we need. You promised that with whatever measure I give, You would cause others to give to me.

I thank You that as I am faithful to pay my tithes and give offering to Your work, You bless me with abundant financial provision. In Jesus' name I pray. Amen.

Scriptures

Honour the Lord with thy substance, and with the firstfruits of all thine increase (Proverbs 3:9).

Bring ye all the tithes into the storehouse, that there may be meat in mine house, and prove me now herewith, saith the Lord of hosts, if I will not open you the windows of heaven, and pour you out a blessing, that there shall not be room enough to receive it. And I will rebuke the devourer for your sakes, and he shall not destroy the fruits of your ground; neither shall your vine cast her fruit before the time in the field, saith the Lord of hosts (Malachi 3:10-11).

Give, and it shall be given unto you; good measure, pressed down, and shaken together, and running over, shall men give into your bosom. For with the same measure that ye mete withal it shall be measured to you again (Luke 6:38).

New Job

Heavenly Father, You put certain desires, gifts, and talents in my nature. Help me to find a job that is a perfect match for me. Provide for me a job that will fulfill and energize me.

Help me to find a job in which I can use my knowledge and gifts to make a difference.

Help me find an employer who will understand my role as a wife and a mother and who will be willing to work with me if I need to be with my family.

Lord, I thank You for a job with good benefits so that I can support all the needs of my family and properly prepare for the future. In Jesus' name I pray. Amen.

Scriptures

Thou hast given him his heart's desire, and hast not withholden the request of his lips (Psalm 21:2).

Having then gifts differing according to the grace that is given to us... (Romans 12:6).

He that diligently seeketh good procureth favour. (Proverbs 11:27).

The hand of the diligent maketh rich (Proverbs 10:4).

Being a Godly Employee

Dear Father, I pray that You would help me to honor You in my job. The Bible says that I can do all things through Christ who strengthens me. I believe that Scripture applies to me on my job.

Let me be a witness to all of my fellow employees as they see Jesus through me. Help me to be bold in my stand for You, Lord.

Let those around me see that I do my work as unto You. For example, I do not abuse the time given to me for lunch or breaks. Help me to also be on time for work and meetings. Help me to keep my commitments and complete all my tasks with excellence and on time. Help me to perform my duties efficiently and effectively. Help me to be the model employee and to constantly look for ways to help the company be profitable and successful.

Let me be a blessing to my fellow employees, to encourage and support them. I put a guard over my mouth so that I will not enter into negative conversations about management, coworkers, or the company. Help me to never complain about my employer but to show the leadership of the company the utmost respect.

May the quality of my work and my faithfulness be a testimony that brings honor to You, Lord. In Jesus' name I pray. Amen.

Scriptures

I can do all things through Christ which strengtheneth me (Philippians 4:13).

Commit thy works unto the Lord, and thy thoughts shall be established (Proverbs 16:3).

Do all things without murmurings and disputings (Philippians 2:14).

Finding the Right Church

Father, in the name of Jesus, I come before You and ask for Your guidance and discernment as I look for the right church for my family and me. Make it clear to me where we are to worship and where we are to serve You. Lord, help me to not be moved by what other people say, by the church's location or convenience, or by the pastor's popularity. Lord, I believe in my heart that You have a specific church that is part of Your plan for the spiritual growth of my family. Direct us to the church of Your choosing where we will worship, receive Your Word, and serve the people. Help me to realize the importance of where we fellowship. Help us to find a home where we can be mentored in our spiritual growth.

I recognize that there are different gifts and talents in different places. Lord, help me to know through Your Word and prayer the exact church that You have for us. In Jesus' name I pray. Amen.

Scriptures

Not forsaking the assembling of ourselves together, as the manner of some is; but exhorting one another: and so much the more, as ye see the day approaching (Hebrews 10:25).

Now there are diversities of gifts, but the same Spirit (1 Corinthians 12:4).

If any of you lack wisdom, let him ask of God, that giveth to all men liberally, and upbraideth not; and it shall be given him (James 1:5).

Before a Church Service

Lord, I come before You with praise and thanksgiving. I worship You and glorify Your name. I come to You concerning this church service in which I am about to participate.

I pray for the speaker. Speak to (his/her) heart. Let the speaker be an instrument of Your Holy Spirit. Minister through (him/her) to the people who will be in the meeting. Help the speaker to be sensitive to Your direction and guidance. Give (him/her) the right words to say as You make the Scripture come alive in (his/her) heart.

I pray for the congregation and myself. Help us to have hearts that are willing and receptive to receive from You. Help us to not be distracted or lose focus during the service. Show us the things You desire us to see. May Your Word reprove, correct, guide, and enlighten us.

I pray that we would be challenged, changed, and edified by the ministry of Your Word. Give us wisdom to practically apply the truth we hear to our daily lives. Strengthen us by the ministry of Your Word. In Jesus' name I pray. Amen.

Scriptures

Enter into his gates with thanksgiving, and into his courts with praise: be thankful unto him, and bless his name (Psalm 100:4).

Preach the word; be instant in season, out of season; reprove, rebuke, exhort with all longsuffering and doctrine (2 Timothy 4:2).

And he gave some, apostles; and some, prophets; and some, evangelists; and some, pastors and teachers; for the perfecting of the saints, for the work of the ministry, for the edifying of the body of Christ (Ephesians 4:11-12).

VIII

Praying For Our Nation

The President

Dear Father, in Jesus' name, I lift up our nation's president to You. I know that our leader's heart is in Your hand, so I ask You to guide the head of our nation in the way You would have him to go.

Give our president spiritual, physical, and mental strength to fulfill his responsibilities with excellence. Give him the courage to stand up for his convictions. Give him patience and peace to endure the pressures of his office.

Help him to be resolute and determined to do the right thing no matter how much pressure he feels from those who oppose him. Grant to our president wisdom and insight concerning every decision that he must make. Give him boldness to lead our nation with integrity and honor.

I pray that You would give our president discernment, understanding, and knowledge so that our nation may know stability, both internally and abroad.

I pray that You would surround our president with wise counsel, godly men and women of integrity who place Your agenda and the good of this nation above their own, people whose motives are pure, honest, and trustworthy.

I pray for our president's family. Encourage and strengthen their spirits, souls, and bodies. Protect them from evil and harm. Help them to be supportive of the president, and give them strength to deal with the pressures and demands of being the First Family.

I give thanks for our president according to Your Word, and thank You for working in and through his leadership so that we might lead peaceable lives in godliness and honesty. In Jesus' name I pray. Amen.

Scriptures

The king's heart is in the hand of the Lord, as the rivers of water: he turneth it whithersoever he will (Proverbs 21:1).

Praying always with all prayer and supplication in the Spirit, and watching thereunto with all perseverance and supplication for all saints; and for me, that utterance may be given unto me, that I may open my mouth boldly, to make known the mystery of the gospel, for which I am an ambassador in bonds: that therein I may speak boldly, as I ought to speak (Ephesians 6:18-20).

I exhort therefore, that, first of all, supplications, prayers, intercessions, and giving of thanks, be made for all men; for kings, and for all that are in authority; that we may lead a quiet and peaceable life in all godliness and honesty (1 Timothy 2:1-2).

Congress

Dear Father, I come to You in the mighty name of Jesus, thanking You and praising You for our great nation. I thank You for the plan You gave to our forefathers to govern our nation and to divide the powers so that our destiny would not rest in the hands of one person.

Because Your Word calls me to pray for those in authority, I lift up our Congress—both the House of Representatives and the Senate. I pray that by Your power, our federal legislative body would make laws that are just.

Father, I ask You to give them wisdom to make decisions that would strengthen and prosper our nation. Enlighten them with Your truth so that they make right decisions concerning the politics, the social welfare, and the economics of our nation.

Help the members of Congress to put aside personal and partisan agendas and to work together with others for the good of our nation. Help them to work with the president so together they can introduce and pass legislation that strengthens our nation and supports the godly values of our society.

I pray for revival in Congress. Draw the representatives of our United States close to You, Lord. Give those who know You the courage to vote their convictions and to be bold witnesses for You to others. For those who don't have a personal relationship with You, I pray that the eyes of their understanding would be opened and their hearts turned toward You. In Jesus' name I pray. Amen.

Scriptures

I exhort therefore, that, first of all, supplications, prayers, intercessions, and giving of thanks, be made for all men; for kings, and for all that are in authority; that we may lead a quiet and peaceable life in all godliness and honesty (1 Timothy 2:1-2).

Therefore he said unto Judah, Let us build these cities, and make about them walls, and towers, gates, and bars, while the land is yet before us; because we have sought the Lord our God, we have sought him, and he hath given us rest on every side. So they built and prospered (2 Chronicles 14:7).

The eyes of your understanding being enlightened; that ye may know what is the hope of his calling, and what the riches of the glory of his inheritance in the saints (Ephesians 1:18).

Military

Thank You, Lord, for the men and women of our armed forces. Protect them as they protect us. Defend them as they defend us. Encourage and strengthen their spirits, souls, and bodies as they perform their duties. May they be mentally and physically strong when required to face the challenges of combat. Undergird them with Your Spirit and might when they are called upon to endure the hardships of battle. Reveal to them the truth and knowledge of Your will for their lives. Help them to be successful in their endeavors, spare their lives from destruction, and deliver them from harm's way.

Father, I come to You concerning the war effort that our nation is currently undertaking. May our response to any aggression by enemies of this nation be swift, accurate, and effective. Reveal the plans, plots, and strategies of our enemies to our military intelligence personnel. Confuse our enemies, and let them become disorganized and disoriented regarding their battle plans.

Father, give our military favor with the governmental agencies of this country. Thank You for providing America with the best-trained and best-equipped military force in the world today. I pray that our Congress would appropriate sufficient funds to keep our nation's military preeminent in the world. In Jesus' name I pray. Amen.

Scriptures

The king's heart is in the hand of the Lord, as the rivers of water: he turneth it whithersoever he will (Proverbs 21:1).

Confuse the wicked, O Lord, confound their speech, for I see violence and strife in the city (Psalm 55:9 NIV).

He keepeth the paths of judgment, and preserveth the way of his saints (Proverbs 2:8).

Our Nation

Father, I thank You for the United States of America. I thank You for the courage, strength, and fortitude of our founding fathers, who set up a new nation based upon the truth and principles of Your Word.

I pray for our nation. I ask You, Lord, to forgive our sins and help us to honor You again. I pray for the leaders of our nation. I pray for spiritual revival in their hearts. Call them unto You, Lord. I pray that they would seek Your counsel and wisdom concerning the issues that face our nation.

I pray for revival across this country. Father God, pour out Your Spirit across the nation. Let the saving knowledge of the Lord Jesus Christ come to every heart, home, and city. Deliver us from our sins, and restore our heritage of faith.

I pray that You would promote godly leadership and remove those in authority who do not honor You. Put a desire in the hearts of Your children to pray for our nation and for our national leaders. Encourage the Christians in our nation to be faithful to vote for and elect godly officials. The United States was once known to the world as a godly nation; help us to regain that position. In Jesus' name I pray. Amen.

Scriptures

If my people, which are called by my name, shall humble themselves, and pray, and seek my face, and turn from their wicked ways; then will I hear from heaven, and will forgive their sin, and will heal their land (2 Chronicles 7:14).

And it shall come to pass in the last days, saith God, I will pour out of my Spirit upon all flesh: and your sons and your daughters shall prophesy, and your young men shall see visions, and your old men shall dream dreams (Acts 2:17).

But it is God who judges: He brings one down, he exalts another (Psalm 75:7 NIV).

I exhort therefore, that, first of all, supplications, prayers, intercessions, and giving of thanks, be made for all men; for kings, and for all that are in authority; that we may lead a quiet and peaceable life in all godliness and honesty (1 Timothy 2:1-2).

National Patriotism

Lord, I thank You for the United States of America. I thank You for the dedication, faith, and fortitude of our founding fathers. I thank You for the patriotism of the generations that have gone before us. I thank You for those brave patriots who have shed their blood for my freedom. Lord, I thank You for all the families who have sacrificed so much so that we might enjoy the liberty we now have.

Now I pray for the people of this generation. Help us to regain the spirit of patriotism that once was the cornerstone of character of all those who called themselves Americans. May our hearts be full of compassion and thankfulness every time we see our flag or hear our national anthem.

I pray that Christians would vote for and elect godly officials. Help us to prayerfully support those who are in authority. Let us teach our children faithfulness, loyalty, and commitment to our country.

Restore to our nation godly character. Promote to positions of authority leaders who will honor You. Let revival and spiritual restoration sweep our country. In Jesus' name I pray. Amen.

Scriptures

I exhort therefore, that, first of all, supplications, prayers, intercessions, and giving of thanks, be made for all men; for kings, and for all that are in authority; that we may lead a quiet and peaceable life in all godliness and honesty (1 Timothy 2:1-2).

When the righteous are in authority, the people rejoice: but when the wicked beareth rule, the people mourn (Proverbs 29:2).

But it is God who judges: He brings one down, he exalts another (Psalm 75:7 NIV).

And it shall come to pass in the last days, saith God, I will pour out of my Spirit upon all flesh: and your sons and your daughters shall prophesy, and your young men shall see visions, and your old men shall dream dreams (Acts 2:17).

National Protection

Most High God, I come to You in prayer asking for divine protection for the people of this nation. I pray for the safety of every man, woman, and child. Keep us from harm's way, and provide protection from plans of destruction that our enemies have plotted. Stop strategies of destruction that our enemies would try to evoke.

Give wisdom, understanding, and discernment to the people who provide protection. Help us as citizens to be watchful and alert to signs of wrongdoing.

Give insight and ideas to inventors and scientists to create better ways to protect our country from financial, political, and mental espionage and terrorism.

Provide insight to national and local authorities to guard, defend, and ensure the safety of all American citizens both at home and abroad. Help us to unite with government leaders and law enforcement personnel in making this country a safe place to live, work, and play. In Jesus' name I pray. Amen.

Scriptures

If my people, which are called by my name, shall humble themselves, and pray, and seek my face, and turn from their wicked ways; then will I hear from heaven, and will forgive their sin, and will heal their land (2 Chronicles 7:14).

I exhort therefore, that, first of all, supplications, prayers, intercessions, and giving of thanks, be made for all men; for kings, and for all that are in authority; that we may lead a quiet and peaceable life in all godliness and honesty (1 Timothy 2:1-2).

Watch and pray, that ye enter not into temptation: the spirit indeed is willing, but the flesh is weak (Matthew 26:41).

Time of War

Father, I come to You in Jesus' name concerning the war effort that our nation is currently undertaking. Give wisdom, insight, and direction to our president and military leaders who are making decisions pertaining to the war.

Reveal the plans, strategies, and inside information about our enemies to our military intelligence personnel. Confuse our enemies. Let them become disorganized and disoriented regarding their battle plans.

I pray that You protect each one of our military personnel involved in the war. Send Your angels to protect them, and go with them to keep them from harm and injury. Encourage and strengthen our armed forces in their spirits, souls, and bodies. Lead them into the truth and knowledge of Your will for their lives. Help them to be successful in their endeavors, spare their lives from destruction, and deliver them from harm's way. In Jesus' name I pray. Amen.

Scriptures

I exhort therefore, that, first of all, supplications, prayers, intercessions, and giving of thanks, be made for all men; for kings, and for all that are in authority; that we may lead a quiet and peaceable life in all godliness and honesty (1 Timothy 2:1-2).

Confuse the wicked, O Lord, confound their speech, for I see violence and strife in the city (Psalm 55:9 NIV).

For he shall give his angels charge over thee, to keep thee in all thy ways (Psalm 91:11).

But let all who take refuge in you be glad; let them ever sing for joy. Spread your protection over them, that those who love your name may rejoice in you (Psalm 5:11 NIV).

God is our refuge and strength, a very present help in trouble (Psalm 46:1).

Other books by Keith & Megan

Scripture Confessions Collection (paperback)

Scripture Confessions Collection (hardback)

Scripture Confessions Dads

Scripture Confessions Finances

Scripture Confessions Healing

Scripture Confessions Moms

Scripture Confessions New Believers

Scripture Confessions Teens

Scripture Confessions Victorious Living

Pray for our Nation

about the authors

KEITH and MEGAN PROVANCE, involved in Christian publishing for more than 40 years, are the founders of Word and Spirit Publishing, a company dedicated to the publishing and worldwide distribution of scriptural, life-changing books. Keith served as president of Harrison House Publishers for more than 20 years and currently works as a publishing consultant to national and international ministries.

Together Keith and Megan have authored a number of bestselling books including: *Scripture Confessions for Moms, Scripture Confessions for Victorious Living, Scripture Confessions for Healing,* and *Pray for Our Nation.*

You may contact Keith & Megan at
Keith@WordandSpiritPublishing.com
Megan@WordandSpiritPublishing.com

Made in the USA
Monee, IL
18 September 2022

14035115R00125